HOLOCAUST STORIES: INSPIRATION FOR SURVIVAL

VOLUME 1
AN ANTHOLOGY

INCLUDING TWO AWARD WINNING STORIES

EDITED BY REBA KARP

Grunwald Publishers

VIRGINIA BEACH, VA • LANCASTER, PA • HOUSTON, TX
LUCERNE, SWITZERLAND

AN ENDORSEMENT FROM CONGRESSMAN TOM LANTOS

At the ground breaking for the U.S. Holocaust Memorial Museum, Elie Wiesel said, "The story we must tell cannot be told—not in its entirety. In our case, the sum of the fragments does not convey the full message. Words, images, memories, prayers, fears, agonies: How does one communicate the burning of a ghetto? Or the arrival of a convoy at Birkenau at midnight? Or the daily massacre of 10,000 men, women, and children, some buried alive, at Babi Yar?"

The enormity of the crimes of the killers may surpass the feeble ability of any language to describe the entire horror, but that does not mean we should not try. The full story of that incredibly brutal and unbelievable crime, and the resistance to it, can never fully be told, but it cannot be forgotten.

This volume of Holocaust remembrances is an important part of that effort. These moving individual accounts by survivors convey on a personal level the horror and tragedy of the darkest episode in human history. Words cannot convey the entirety of this ultimate example of man's inhumanity, but these personal recollections do give us a glimpse of the whole.

As a survivor of the Holocaust, I have shared many of the experiences and feelings that are recounted in this book. It is important—though it is often painful and incomplete—to remember through the eyes and hearts of survivors, the depth of the horror of these events.

Remembering and trying to understand that tragedy is not enough. We can do nothing now for those who were slaughtered. But we can—and must—be certain they are not forgotten. More importantly, we must commit ourselves to create conditions that will prevent the repetition of this darkest episode in human history. It must never happen again.

Congressman Tom Lantos
(D) San Mateo, California

(The Publishers gratefully thank Congressman Lantos for his endorsement and cooperation in supporting this book.)

Congressman Tom Lantos is the only survivor of the Holocaust to be elected to Congress. Born in Budapest, Hungary, he was twice sent to Nazi work camps, but escaped and survived through the efforts of Raoul Wallenberg. Lantos was active in the anti-Nazi underground. He came to the United States in 1947 and has lived in the San Francisco Bay area since 1950. He married Annette Tillemann, his childhood sweetheart, who also was born in Budapest and also survived the Holocaust through Wallenberg's efforts.

HOLOCAUST STORIES: INSPIRATION FOR SURVIVAL

VOLUME 1

Library of Congress Cataloging-in-Publication Data

Holocaust stories. Inspiration For Survival

Bibliography: p.
1. Holocaust, Jewish (1939-1945)--Personal
narratives. I. Karp, Reba.
D810.J4H658   1985   940.53'15'03924 85-30567
ISBN 0-915133-14-8
ISBN 0-915133-13-X (pbk.)

Manufactured by Apollo Books, 107 Lafayette St., Winona, MN 55987

PRINTED IN THE UNITED STATES OF AMERICA

Judaica Books and Media Productions: A Series (Number 1)

This series is respectfully dedicated to DAVID BEN-GURION

The Publishers are creating a major series of book and audio/video projects devoted, in the spirit of Ben-Gurion, to Jewish affairs, life, culture, religion, history, and current and future developments. The thrust of this series is to enlighten and educate Jewish and non-Jewish children alike, but there are many ways for adolescents and adults to be involved. The Publishers hope Jews will discover renewed pride in themselves by participating in these projects and non-Jews will learn about, and gain appreciation for, the joys and sufferings of their numerous fellow Jewish citizens. It is our fervent wish that most of the series' projects will create an in-depth closeness and ecumenism among people of all faiths. We hope to play a modest part, among the many other Jewish and non-Jewish enlightened people, organizations, fellow publishers, etc. in bringing about an international renaissance of mutual love, appreciation, tolerance, respect for human rights, and "a let us live together peaceably" attitudes, all of which are borne out of Ben-Gurion's spirit and dreams, realized with strength, determination, vision and pragmatism.

Editor in Chief
Reba Karp

The Publishers are assembling an international Editorial Board, to be assisted by an Advisory Board, and will soon announce the selection of a chairperson for each board. We are soliciting suggestions for individuals to serve on these boards, as well as manuscripts to be considered as projects for this series. Please write to us at the address below.

For information, write:
Grunwald Publishers,
5049 Admiral Wright Road, Suite 344,
Virginia Beach, Va. 23462

This book has been co-sponsored by Andrew M. Fekete, M.D. It is being published as a fund raising effort on behalf of the United Jewish Federation of Tidewater, with funds earmarked for the erection of a Holocaust memorial and a library. Publishers gratefully acknowledge Dr. Fekete's sponsorship and the cordial and active co-operation of the U.J.F.T.

Ten stories anthologized here appeared in three Holocaust Supplements published by the United Jewish Federation of Tidewater. They are being reprinted by permission, for which the Publishers give sincere thanks. One, *The Broken Hour*, is reprinted by special permission from the author's agent.

AWARD WINNING STORIES

The story *The Broken Hour* was honored with the literary prize of the Province of Antwerp, 1980. The Dutch original now appears in a special school edition.

The story *Memories of a Lost Childhood* won first place in the feature writing category in a competition sponsored by the Virginia Press Women, Inc., 1985.

TABLE OF CONTENTS

Editor's Foreword

The biographical sketches in *Holocaust Stories: Inspiration For Survival, VOL. 1* (an anthology containing **two award winning stories**) challenge you to break the puzzling code of survival—why did 6 million perish and yet how did a select few manage to survive? Those who did survive will inspire you and give you pointers on how to uplift yourself in times of troubles and to go on and live a better, richer life.

On your odyssey into a time warp which defies acceptance, you meet, among others, Stefan, a child of the Holocaust, growing up in the streets, running from the Germans; and Dvorah, the young Jewish mother, outside the camps with her young child, as she sought to survive in a world where every move was suspect and her every word guarded. Forged papers and an indomitable will to live were her passport to freedom.

On one hand these stories represent memories out of the dark—the hidden place where nightmares originate, made even more compelling in that they portray fact not fiction. On the other hand, these stories challenge one to never let the horrors of tyranny and violation of human rights happen again. They also teach the inspirational lesson of survival. Also, do these horrors echo a not too distant past, or are they forerunners of a yet more devastating future—for the entire world?

There are lessons to be learned from this book, and one is unable to leave the people portrayed in this volume without having learned through them about the Holocaust, hate-fostered prejudice and survival. It is for this reason also that educators are asking for this book as a text for school children, and that Christian lay teachers are recommending it for use in study groups. At least one television producer wants to use the stories for a series of video shows.

Publishers' Note:

This anthology is not intended to continue the sensationalization of the Hitler experience. Rather, in speaking with Eli Wiesel, it is meant to enhance the educational process for Jews and Gentiles, which according to Wiesel, is the foremost tool for the prevention of another outbreak of anti-Semitism. It is thus our sincere wish that this volume will become part of children's and young adults' reading study, for history is still the best teacher. (A separate study apparatus is available from the Publishers.) In a most important sense, also, we hope that this book will join those publications which inveigh against the violation of human rights of any people, race or creed. The process of violation is the same, as is the pernicious outcome.

Furthermore, as this anthology contains materials for video productions, we hope that some story will catch the eye of a TV/motion picture director. The wider distribution the message can find, the better we will all be. Last but not least, it is our wish that you the reader, of whatever age and state in life, will be impacted by the fact that: no matter how hard a life can be; how cruelly you may have permitted yourself to have been dealt with by others; however much you may have lost; you can survive and carry on with your existence, particularly if you permit your God to assist you. The inspiration for this is given by the people depicted.

We humbly thank the survivors written about in these pages for going through the usually torturous experience of recall, and permitting others to share. We salute them for having survived and prevailed.

Our gratitude goes out also to the Tidewater, Virginia United Jewish Federation for sponsoring the original publication of most stories. Also, our deep-felt appreciation goes out to Dr. Andrew Fekete, who together with the Publishers, co-sponsored the publication of this volume.

Special thanks also to Mr. Abraham Liess, Post 379 Commander; Mr. Arthur L. Eppner, Old Dominion Post 158; and to Mrs. Ruth Fekete, formerly executive secretary, Auxiliary, National Office, Jewish War Veterans of the United States of America, for their advice regarding this book and its possibilities.

Responses From School Children and a Teacher

(Publisher's Note: The responses below come from a class of 7th graders who in May, 1985 were visited by Mrs. A. Friedman (a Survivor), and Mrs. R. Fekete in the course of their regular school visits, aimed at teaching children about the Holocaust.

[Following are excerpts from two letters by the teacher, Mrs. D.D.S.]:

"Dear Mrs. Friedman: The students were stunned by you. Seeing you was like all of the pages they've studied coming to life...**Very little catches and holds their attention. You were able to do that!** They admire you because you've taught them something in a way we can't always reach them. You showed sensitivity...I know I can never feel the pain that you feel, but I did share a little of your pain...I learned that when we hurt others it doesn't simply just go away. It stays and it doesn't just hurt one person. Because we all in one way or another feel the pain and it affects all of our lives...I will truly never forget you.

"Dear Mrs. Fekete: The students wrote the letters [below]...I felt they were really speaking from the heart and wanted you to know their true feelings. **They very seldom seem interested in anything, and I have to say they haven't stopped talking about you!**...Often this year I've had to get after them to be considerate and kind. I think I've seen something different in them and I am happy to say you brought about this change. Thank God for people like you!"

[Following are uncorrected excerpts from letters by the children to both speakers:]

"We appreciate the lesson you helped us to learn."
"I will never forget what we heard from you."
"I learned a lot from it. I'm glad you are still livening [sic.]"
"It was sad when you cried...I put my head down. I felt hurt when you cried."

"I learn a lot and am sorry your life had to be like that but now you have freedom. I felt sorry about mom and dad dying."

"I'm very sorry that you could not see your parents before they died."

"...we know it was hard to talk about mother and father."

"I am very sad for you but I hope you live a better life here in this country."

"You taught us about World War II. We will never forget the lesson we learned."

"I know it was very hard for you to speak about it. Thank you."

"I learned a lot. We would like to learn more about it. Thank you very, very much."

EACH DAY...A DAWN OF NEW HORRORS
Bluma Kushner Bromberg

By Reba Karp

Bluma Kushner Bromberg is an attractive impeccably dressed woman. Her entire appearance bespeaks of a quiet and dignified life-style.

But it is a facade, for while many of her contemporaries in America and other Western countries were in college or getting married and setting up homes, she was confined in ghettos and labor and concentration camps.

She speaks softly, covering up insecurities which she admits are hard to keep in check when the memories of those years take over.

"I am nervous," she said softly before letting herself go back to times she would rather forget. But she feels she has a responsibility to future generations and to the world at large to record her story, for she doesn't believe the truth of what happened is totally believed by all; for indeed, weren't the crimes in themselves totally incomprehensible to the civilized millennium? she questions.

"I wanted to escape, but where could I go? I never believed people could do so much to other people and not feel something...although I wished many times not to get up in the morning, I wanted to survive to tell others what it feels like to be a Jew," she said.

Consequently, no matter how torturous her life became, she never entertained the notion of taking her own life, and what truly kept her going was the hope that she would survive to belie the German's oft-spoken threat that "no Jews will be alive in the future."

Although she wanted to live, she did not fear death, for it was commonplace. As penned on November 20, 1942 in a diary of "E.K." found in liberated Dachau, "these pages that I now begin to write would lead to certain death if they were found. But what is death? How few of those I knew here are still alive today, how close to death we all stand. I can die here any moment even if I take the greatest care…Why should I not endeavor, even in the midst of these conditions of this cruelty, to tell this gruesome story that no longer gives us goose flesh?"

And so Bluma Kushner Bromberg tells her story of an odyssey in hell.

Before the war she lived near Vilna, Poland with her brothers and sisters. In all there were seven, including her parents—a happy middle-class Jewish family. Her father, who was a merchant, owned farmland which he rented to Polish farmers. She was about 16 or 17 years old when she got her introduction to German cruelty—the systematic search and seizure of property from the Jewish population.

What could they do as they stood and watched their possessions become the property of the Third Reich? To speak up, to protest, would earn the butt of a rifle blow on the face, in the stomach. So they watched in quiet, sober fear. At first, the Germans settled for Jewish plunder and when there was nothing else left to take, they went for Jewish blood.

"They took property first and later took people…not all at once, but in small groups." Those who did protest or those they did not want to take "they killed, just threw them on the streets and shot them."

Her painful journey through horror began when she and members of her family were brutally tossed on trucks and transported to the ghetto. She remembers: "Five families in one room…maybe 18 people, no sanitary conditions…children crying, squeezed in, sleeping on the floor…"

Some tried to escape, to get across the border to Russia. Those caught were beaten to death.

Punishment for those living in the ghettos was special "just because we were Jews," she said, recalling the hours they were forced to stand barefoot in winter in swamp water while they bore the brunt of brute cruelty. "To save bullets they would throw small children (those a year and younger) against tree trunks," she said, where they were left, dead and dying. The children's mothers were forced to bear witness as they stood helplessly in line.

Those taken outside the ghetto for work details, never knew if they would return. "We thought, if we could die a normal death, it would be a blessing." The first in her family to succumb was her father, who died of a heart attack while living in the ghetto. Later her brother would be killed while trying to escape.

And as their emotions became numb, they tried to gather strength from within. "We could not believe it, we waited day by day, maybe it would disappear."

Ghetto life for her and her family ended as abruptly as it began. Two groups were selected. Her group went to a labor camp. The other was stuffed into box cars and burned alive, she later learned.

What remained of her family, two sisters, a younger brother and her mother began a new countdown of days in hard labor. "We had to lay stones for roads, using mallets and picks." The fate of those unable to work is well-known—beaten with the butt of rifles or shot in the head.

No one had enough food, even the SS men in charge of the laborers. So she survived by begging food from neighboring farms for herself and her German captors. "We couldn't run away, for where would we go?" she questions as she explains her reason for returning to the camp.

Although they reasoned it wasn't much, it was an existence. Surely the war would end and sanity would reign once again.

One day in particular stand out in Bluma's mind—the day she last saw her mother and younger brother. The call was out for mothers with small children to assemble for transport to Auschwitz. They clung together, but only for a moment before her mother pushed Bluma and her sisters away. She would not hear of their going with her, for she believed that by parting it would increase their chances of survival. Later Bluma would be separated from her sisters at Stutthof.

But, before they parted, Stutthof would dawn with new horrors. Before being introduced into the camp's already existing population, the new inmates were deloused and deprived of their clothing and personal items. Then they were issued new clothing, which in many instances was to further humiliate them rather than cover their bodies.

"So many had been killed in Stutthof," Bluma said, that a casual shifting of the foot in the ground would unearth a tooth, a bone or a shoe from someone burned and buried. She was in Stutthof from February to June of 1944.

Before Bluma reached Stutthof however, she was literally dragged on foot from one place to another as the Germans sought to escape the advancing Russians. It was during this interval that she slept out in the open wherever she fell, unless they found a barn, or were in temporary camps and behind barbed wire.

In June of 1944 she was transferred to another labor camp from Stutthof and forced to work on roads once more until she was liberated in May of 1945.

When liberated by the Russians she was living in barracks in a forest. "More than half were already dead, lying next to the living. This I will never forget as long as I live."

Many lived to be liberated, only to die shortly afterward of dysentery caused by trying to eat food their systems were not ready to digest. Although liberation had been a much dreamed of moment for Bluma, as well as for many others, it proved to be a let down. "I questioned if it were true, if it was really over, I didn't want to be alive. I didn't have anyone."

And she had nowhere to go. When she regained some of her strength, a Jewish man in the Russian army helped her and a few other women to return to Poland where she encountered another brutal disappointment in the form of a band of murderous Poles and Germans who were still determined to kill Jewish people even though the war was over. So she fled once more. "I didn't know where I was going. I was just moving, looking for a safe haven until I could get to Israel."

In Lodz she met her first husband Saul Kushner, also a survivor, and they were married. Later they decided to move to Norfolk because Kushner had family living there. "My first husband escaped a pre-mature ghetto grave by digging his way through dirt and dead bodies and then joined the partisans. He took part in raids against the Germans and Poles," she said.

Until they moved to Norfolk, the Kushners lived in Belgium where her daughter Irene was born. Irene is married to Joseph Weintrab and they have two children, 9 and 4. Saul Kushner died several years ago. Bluma married Alexander Bromberg in 1983.

Both of Bluma's sisters survived and are now living in Israel. One, she said, returned after the war to Poland for a brief stay, living with her uncle who was later killed by a Pole.

"I will never return to Poland even if they gave me a free ticket...not even for a million dollars will I ever return," she concluded.

A YAHRZEIT IN WORDS
Harry Bromberg

By Reba Karp

Yehiel De Nur, a survivor of Auschwitz, who has written five books on the subject, among them *House of Dolls*, chooses to write under his concentration number Ka-Tzetnik 135633. The reason is simplistic and is based on a special need for identification, for he notes: "My name, Ka-Tzetnik 135633 is not just a pen name—I see myself as a chronicler from the planet of Auschwitz..."

Another survivor, Harry Bromberg of Tidewater expresses his "pain at being liberated" in similar terms. With liberation and relief came fragile joy—and how could it be expressed other than fragile in a person weighing only 75 pounds and suffering from malnutrition, mental exhaustion and lack of identity? When the joy of liberation subsided, he looked around for a familiar face or landmark and walked into a dead end. He had survived six years in hell, while his family had been erased, his roots annihilated.

He had become an alien on his own planet. "The question was, where will I go? I had no one else in the world."

The liberation became a bittersweet victory. "My family perished in Treblinka." A few almost made it to the finish line. "My brother and his son hid in a hole in a village during the war. They were killed three days before liberation. My youngest brother, he was only 13 years old, was killed in a similar manner, while hiding, sold out by the Poles."

He wants to tell his story, a yahrzeit in words. Before the war he worked in Warsaw in a small shoe factory where tips for shoes were made and where leather was processed for sale to shoemakers. His family lived in Stanislaw, 40 kilometers away. The year was 1939.

"When the Germans marched in, they took all the young Jewish people and locked them in a church for three days. We had no food, no water, no facilities."

His words are Spartan and he rushes through events as if speed can diminish the pain of remembering. When the Germans finally opened the door to the church, they began the systematic mental and physical abuse of the young Jewish people which was to characterize the Third Reich and stigmatize an entire generation.

"They tried to cut off the beards of the religious with their bayonets," he said, adding that they also struck the now weakened and unprotected bodies with their rifles and inflicted whatever torture was at their disposal.

He fared better than most. "They got me to work, pushing trucks. The roads were impossible for trucks to get by." But he realized he could not long endure, for his captors viewed him merely as a Jewish body without a man inside. And as such, he was only to be used until he could not be used any longer.

He tried to escape several times, finally getting across the river to Byelorussia, Russian-occupied Poland. He and a friend made it to Stolpcy where they worked in a factory until 1941, living in the field, men without an address. "We were caught in the middle. We were refugees. We did not have any home."

But his restricted freedom was short for when the Germans arrived, they sought out the Jewish people and put them in ghettos, a panorama of horror, punctuated by the knowledge there was nowhere to run.

He recalls the time when the Germans put a call out for all the ghetto Jewish children. "The mothers who didn't want to give up their children were bayoneted, other children were thrown from five to six stories up onto the trucks below."

Conditions were crowded, food was scarce, if at all, and death was commonplace. Although it was routine to evacuate Jews from the ghettos for mass executions and massacres, no one became apathetic. The will to survive kept many alive. He was later transferred to a smaller ghetto in Dworez, where his profession as a shoemaker spared him. "After we were led out, the rest, the women and children were killed," he said.

"We were taken away, in box cars, to a work camp in Krasny Bor" (Red Forest). There his job was to mend the shoes taken off dead and wounded German soldiers. "Some still contained part of the foot or toes of the last to wear the shoes," he remembered.

His grizzly task was made all the more difficult by the imposition of a quota, which if he fell behind, earned him 100 lashes, administered with an instrument of torture similar to three water hoses tied together with wire. "I still have some of the scars," he said quietly.

"Rations were a small loaf of bread for 10 people and soup made with water and sawdust. Many caught dysentery and died."

Other memories of Krasny Bor are living nightmares which return at unsuspecting moments. "During count each morning as we stood in the snow, we were hosed down with water," and "I saw potato peelings in the latrine. I was so hungry, I dug them out."

When the Russians broke through the German lines, he was once more placed in a railroad box car with 120 other humans, without food, water and sanitary conditions for 14 days and 14 nights. The cars only moved by night; during the day they were at a standstill by the side of the road or at a railroad station. It was summer. "At the stations, we would beg the Poles for a little water. The reply was always the same. 'You damn Jews. You're soon going to fry in a crematorium.' We were not far from Auschwitz," he said.

"I feel the Germans put their most infamous camps in Poland because of the Polish people. They had organized groups called Endeks who grabbed Jewish people off the street and beat upon them."

By the time the box car reached its destination about 70 percent had perished. Due to lack of space some of the dead were still in an upright position when the doors were opened. There was no room for them to slide down, for they had been shoved up against one another for Teutonic expediency, as if inanimate objects and not human beings.

In 1942 Bromberg found himself at Majdanek, where once more his profession as a shoemaker spared his life. The scene was a familiar one when he arrived—the shoemakers, laborers and carpenters were herded into one group—all the others went to the crematorium.

"Thoughts centered on getting enough to eat and drink. We didn't have the strength to commit suicide. No one thought they would ultimately survive. The goal was to live one more day. Those who lacked the desire for that one more day, threw themselves on the electric barbed wire which circled the camp."

Even in the midst of their struggle to survive, the Jewish people tried to establish a system among themselves in which rules prevailed. Bromberg remembers incidents in Blyzn to support this inner striving for order. "We worked repairing and making shoes…quotas had to be met, food was very little." But what they had was evenly distributed. Portions were weighed as best as they could be. And in order to avoid arguments, all portions were cut and distributed as each turned his or her back. "This way no one could say another had gotten a larger share."

An epidemic of typhus broke out while he was in Blyzn. "Hundreds died. Our barrack, number nine was on a hill. I had to crawl on my belly to reach it. I didn't have the strength to walk." When the strength to crawl on his belly finally failed him, he was tossed into the "hospital barrack," an enclosure where the dead and dying lay indiscriminately one upon another. "I was on the floor, covered with dead bodies...I tried to crawl over them." What was left of his strength grew less with each futile movement. He was trapped in a web of arms, hands, legs and hair of the dead and dying.

A hand reached out. Someone pulled him from the pile and placed him upon a platform. "Somehow I survived." The same man, one he refers to as a "doctor" brought him a little food, a little soup. "I don't know why or how. He appeared so tall. Even after I was released from the hospital, he told me to come back and see him, that he would give me part of his food."

"It was like God, I had to live."

After the war, Bromberg tried to find the man who had miraculously saved his life. He had disappeared as strangely as he had appeared.

From Blyzn he was transferred to Crakow and from Crakow to Mauthausen where he was subjected to two weeks on quarantine—a system of further inhumane treatments. The men were kept completely naked...forced to sit between each other's legs. It was back-to-back torture. Bromberg recalls that in an inhuman effort to get the Jewish men closer together during the initial line-up, German soldiers would hit each man in the stomach in an effort to get him to pull in tighter.

And so they sat through the night, not only unable to find a restful position in which to sleep, but unable to move any limb beyond a limited area. To some sleep came in the nightshades of death.

As the Russians approached in 1944, the inmates were marched to Ebaenze, Austria. Those who couldn't walk, were shot. Bromberg learned later that the people in a previous transport had been put on a boat which was deliberately gutted so the Jews on board would drown.

Ebaenze, which was surrounded by mountains, "was like being in a hole. We felt, as we looked around, God cannot find us here."

The Jewish people died by the thousands at Ebaenze, Bromberg said, "The crematoriums couldn't burn them fast enough. Many were buried outside the fence."

But the dwindling number of survivors held on. Liberation was not far away.

"We were warned not to go if the Germans wanted to put us in an underground shelter where ammunition was made," he said, explaining that the very next day the German soldiers tried to coax them into the shelter, telling them it was for their own safety.

"We refused to go, we knew we were going to be blown up." Consequently, the Germans were ready to machine gun the inmates when the American tanks broke through. The Germans on the guard tower were killed, others surrendered.

"We ran out, even kissed the tanks," he said, remembering that after the initial jubilation, reality took over. "We had lost everything. We were left with the feeling that life was not worth living...I didn't have anyone. I didn't have anywhere to go."

The Americans gave him food, which he tried to eat, although his system wasn't ready for food. "I felt like I was dying. They took me to the hospital, I remember, even now, they gave me medicine which smelled like turpentine."

Later, he married his wife, Paula, who was liberated 30 miles from him, in a displaced persons camp. When his wife got pregnant, he realized it would be difficult for them to get to Israel and he turned to an uncle in America for assistance. He wrote letters to every Jewish newspaper as well as other American newspapers looking for his uncle, asking his help. By chance his uncle read of his plight and helped him get to America.

The Brombergs have two children, a daughter, Dr. Susan Bromberg Schneider who lives in St. Louis with her husband, Dr. Robert Schneider, and a son Al Bromberg, who is now living in Little Rock, Arkansas. The Brombergs also have three grandchildren.

Even now, many years after liberation, Bromberg finds it difficult to sleep through the night without painful dreams.

But despite the horror which returns in his dreams, "I still believe in God," he said. He is a Survivor.

HER MEMORIES:
A PANORAMA OF HORROR
Esther Goldman

By Reba Karp

Esther Goldman is a survivor—a special individual with the indomitable ability to withstand adverse conditions and end up on her feet. But she is more. She is among the dwindling number of Jewish people who were victimized by the Holocaust.

An attractive woman, who speaks positively, she is not unlike other women who are neat and well-dressed. The one obvious exception are the numbers she has tattooed on her left arm. She does not try to conceal them, for they are testimony that she is a special person—that she is a Jewish survivor of Hitler's "Final Solution."

She was born in Sokoly, Poland in 1924—before half of the world went mad. Among her earliest recollections of her childhood are fear and a life punctuated by hiding, which began when her mother sent her each evening to the home of an elderly Jewish couple. Here, she would spend the night, hiding from the Germans "who pulled young Jewish girls from their homes and raped them and God knows what else," she said.

Later, she and other young Jewish people of her town, were to spend many long days working for the German army, making an inflammable product she describes as similar to charcoal briquets. This was in 1939.

Then on the eve of Rosh Hashana in 1940 or 1941, the Germans had a new idea—they decided to burn down Jewish homes, and her family's was among them. She remembers a plane flying low over the town early one morning, her mother was baking bread. The plane, she feels, was a signal, for shortly thereafter, Jewish homes began to burn. Her family escaped out of the back door, and spent Rosh Hashana eve hiding in a cemetery. In the morning when they returned to sift through the ashes of their home, they

met some of their Jewish neighbors who had not managed to escape—their
bodies littered the streets.

Temporary refuge was found with another Jewish family, and life, for
the Jews who were left, trudged on in Sokoly until 1942 when they heard a
rumor that the Jewish people were going to be sent away. "In the evening
we decided to hide. The roads were not blocked and we hid in the forest.
Those who did not leave…they killed."

She remembers a night in the forest made light from the fire of German
rifles and German spotlights. In the confusion, she was separated from her
family. "I was all alone. I saw a neighbor, I went up to him and asked if he
would take me along with him." Esther's mother had tried to prepare her
family of 10 for this moment, for the ordeal of survival. Each child was
given some of her jewelry which they were to exchange for help or food.
Additionally, Esther wore as many garments as possible, which she could
shed to help ransom herself. An outer garment bought her the privilege of
hiding with 16 other Jews in an underground excavation where potatoes had
been previously stored.

"I'm scratching now," she said, "because I remember the lice…we were
two weeks with lice and no water to bathe…16 people in a little lousy
grave. We were almost buried alive."

One night stands out in her mind now. "We heard footsteps, there were
two children, one was my brother. How they found the place I don't know.
He asked me if I had something left that mother had given me. I had a
bracelet. I gave it to him."

Before he left she learned that her mother and other sisters and brothers
were dead. "My mother gave all she had to Christian people to save the two
youngest. I later learned that they turned the children over to the Nazis," she
added.

Jewish children grew up fast in Poland in those days. Her younger
brother, already wise in the battle of survival, told Esther that if she wanted
to leave the "grave" to go to the synagogue in the city where the Jews who
were captured were herded. And when she could no longer stand being
"buried alive" she followed his advice. "The Germans came to the synagogue
and locked us up at night in case anyone had any idea about escaping. It was
the first time I was in jail." The next morning they were taken by train to
the ghetto in Byalistok.

At the ghetto she found two of her brothers, one the same who sought her in the forest. But it was no happy family reunion for they were unable to live together. For awhile she eked out survival by working as a seamstress in a factory making military clothing for the Germans.

"Then early one morning, when I awoke there was no one in the house where I lived. I could hear screaming and shouting and Germans in the streets. Everyone was running to hide, it was everyone for himself. I didn't know what to do, no one wanted to take me along," she said, remembering that she returned to the attic where she slept. A strange woman was there. She had a bag of dried beans. "It was the only food we had." The woman's last name was Pincus. In their fear and need for someone else, they decided they would face what was before them as sisters.

Since they could not remain hiding forever, they eventually found themselves on a cattle train to Birkenau. "The doors were slammed...I don't recall how long we rode. We were so squeezed we couldn't turn around. Babies were laying dead...the stench."

Then the doors opened. A day not much unlike many other days—except that Mengele was there and giving orders. "One to the left, one to the right. I spotted my sister-in-law and I started to run towards her. I got hit on the head and forced to go left."

Then the organized torture of the German Third Reich begun to unfold. The prisoners were ordered to undress and their heads and bodies shaved. She will never forget the humiliation, she said. They were given old clothes and forced into quarters already overcrowded—shoved into a dark room with the dead, the dying and those determined to survive. There was no where to lay, no wall to lean against, scarcely any place to stand and no familiar object to touch for orientation. Just the darkness and the nameless. "We just survived that night." In the morning they were lined up for count, five in a row. It was a regular procedure. "If someone was missing we had to stand for hours until that person was accounted for."

Her block number was 15 and she remembers the terror vividly. The nights were dark and the light of day revealed those who had died during the night. The lucky ones had a blanket, those who didn't would try to steal one or wait and take it from those dead. "Death was commonplace. We pulled them (the bodies) out in the morning…wagons would carry them away," she said.

"I worked out of the camp in the field. I had an old coat. I was told to reverse it and fill the front with rocks and debris. We reversed the procedure the next day." The march to the fields and back to camp was another exercise in survival. "The dogs killed those unable to march back to camp." The routine was basically the same for six days each week. Ironically they were not forced to "work" on Sunday. "I don't know why," she said.

Events pass through her memory as a panorama of horror. "The camp hospital was a dreaded place. Once you were in, you were lucky to come out alive…it was a place you'd pray to God you'd die…"

Then she remembers the "showplace" for the Red Cross. Here, men, women and children and humane conditions were paraded in front of the Red Cross to dupe them. "Then afterwards they made us dig graves…they put the children inside and gave them toys to pacify them, poured something over them and burned them alive."

She was later transferred to Auschwitz where she was selected to work in an ammunition factory. "Conditions were a little better. If you made your quota, you got a slice of bread, a piece of margarine…the bread was so dear."

Another memory. "There were no children in Auschwitz. One woman was pregnant. They let her have the baby, then killed her and took the infant to experiment on it."

In 1945 as the war drew to an end they were forced to march to Ravensbrück. They were transported deep into Germany where their work once more consisted of "silly things." Then early in May the routine suddenly changed. "They let us out one morning. There were carrots lying in the field. We shoved all we could into our clothes to have something to eat." Then later they were put into their blocks, which were locked from the outside. "We were frightened. We looked out in the evening. The guards were gone. We somehow managed to get out, but not before crying and screaming. We feared they were going to burn us to death."

Once out, they found they were alone. No Germans. They searched the soldiers' barracks. They were empty. "We knew the Germans were running," she said. They broke into a warehouse for food and then returned to their blocks and barricaded the doors "and waited for someone to liberate us. We prayed to God…isn't it strange that we still believed in God?"

But no one came to liberate them. So they decided to march, thinking "the highway would take us someplace." By the time they reached a town, the German citizens were frightened and offered them no resistance. They went into a bakery and took the bread, and what they couldn't eat themselves, they destroyed so no one else could.

After more trials, the band of camp refugees were given a horse and wagon from a Russian officer and they set out again. "Where we were going, I don't know." But since all roads must end somewhere, they eventually met Polish Jewish soldiers who took care of them, telling their officers that they had found lost relatives. Of course, Esther notes, the officers knew it was only a ploy so they could help the survivors.

Esther, who has lived in the Tidewater, Virginia area since 1957, is married to Charles Goldman, another Holocaust survivor. They have two grown sons. She feels her story must be told and doesn't like the idea that it may be shortened. "Can you imagine four years of life being told in a few hours?" she questions.

"Now at night when I sleep I am running, trying to hide my children. In my mind I go through more than you can put on paper.

"More hell I don't think anyone can endure. When I awaken in the morning and realize that I am still alive, I feel it is a miracle."

ANONYMITY INCREASED THEIR CHANCES OF SURVIVAL
Ann Friedman

By Valerie Freeman Samsell

You are the most beautiful daughters in all the world," Isaac Altenhaus whispered as he stroked his daughters' long flowing hair.

For Anneke and Mina, those wonderful carefree days of childhood would soon end, and only the memories of indescribable terror would endure.

Antwerp, Belgium was a peaceful metropolis where Gentiles and Jews lived side-by-side in friendship. The Altenhaus family enjoyed a quiet, happy life. Isaac Altenhaus, a custom tailor, was a good family provider, while Pepi his devoted wife, took pride in her role as a "Jewish Mother." Their daughters Anneke and Mina were happy children whose days were filled with childhood play.

On May 10, 1939, Germany invaded Belgium. Storm troopers goose-stepped, robot-like through the streets of Antwerp, filling the hearts of its citizens with fear and despair.

Years before the invasion, Pepi felt the need to uproot her family and move them to America. Her already unbearable anxiety was constantly increasing because of the countless horror stories related by Jewish refugees fleeing Nazi persecution. Papa, however, refused to leave because Uncle Oscar in America wrote only about hard times there. He reminded them with pride that Belgium had been good to them; they enjoyed prosperity, freedom, security.

Three weeks after the Nazis invaded Antwerp, Pepi once again sensed the urgency to leave Europe and this time convinced Isaac to flee. Within the hour, they packed everything they could carry and set out on foot for France and freedom.

After several hours, they came to a schoolyard filled with hundreds of refugees. Some slept on filthy cobblestones while babies cried and women wept. Little Mina coughed all night and in the morning Pepi decided to return to their home in Antwerp. At least there she was surrounded by the security of her beloved home. After all, what could be worse than sleeping in schoolyards on cobblestones with hundreds of strangers?

For Anneke, 10 years old, and Mina, 7, this was to be the first of a series of attempted escapes that would eventually lead to freedom.

Isaac took pride in his work as a custom tailor. He specialized in tailoring uniforms for the Antwerp Police Department. This specialization led the Nazis to insist on his manufacturing Nazi uniforms. Despite his dislike for the task, Isaac had no choice but to comply. At that time the Germans did not know he was Jewish.

Life went on as tension filled the city of Antwerp. Then in 1941, the harassment of Jewish citizens began in earnest. Jews were forced to identify themselves by wearing the yellow Star of David on their coats. Then came the closing of Jewish businesses and ordinances forbidding Jews in public places or public functions. These included the theater, parks, and even the trolley cars. A gathering of two or more Jews was considered a criminal offense as was being on the streets from 7 p.m. to 7 a.m. Finally, there was the deportation of Jewish men to what they presumed were "labor camps."

On a Wednesday afternoon in June 1942 Isaac, then 44 years old, received a notice that he was to report to the railroad station in Antwerp for deportation to a work camp. Anneke, who was then 12 years old remembered that the father of a close schoolmate was a Nazi collaborator and in charge of the list of attendance at the station. It was a gamble but the family decided to hurry through the streets of Antwerp before the curfew was enacted, and ask the man to strike Isaac from the list. Isaac, Pepi and Anneke stood fearlessly in the collaborator's home, pleading and crying for him to postpone Isaac's deportation.

"Go home," he said. "Don't worry, your name will not be called."

Luckily, Isaac and Pepi had money saved which could buy them a little more time. They were now convinced that they must leave their home and hide until the war was over.

In August of 1942, Isaac brought the bolts of cloth from his business over to the home of Janine Zurich, a school chum of Anneke. An arrangement was then made to keep the goods there until someone could come for them.

The separation would be difficult, but there was no room for an entire family to hide. The girls went to live in the country and Isaac and Pepi stayed in the suburbs of Antwerp, hidden by friends.

The country was beautiful in August, but Anneke and Mina found it hard to adjust to a lifestyle so unfamiliar to them. They stayed with an elderly couple and played the part of Christian sisters who came to the country for reasons of poor health. Since Jews were forbidden to attend school, the couple felt that suspicions would be aroused if the girls were not enrolled in September when the school year began. Overcome with fear, they contacted Isaac and Pepi and arranged for the girls to go back to their parents in the suburbs.

A family friend came to the country to bring Anneke and Mina to Antwerp. On the train ride back, Gestapo agents roamed the aisles demanding passports from everyone. Miraculously, Anneke and Mina were passed by and their hearts then began to beat normally again.

Isaac and Pepi occupied one of four bedrooms on the second floor of their friend's home. An entrance foyer made up the entire first floor. The living room and kitchen were in the basement, and a small courtyard housed an opaque glass watercloset with an open urinal nearby.

On a rainy October morning in 1942, three Nazi officers appeared at the front door. The Altenhaus family was gathered in the basement when their friend opened the door.

"Heil fraulein! We have orders to search your house!" demanded the German officer. "It has been reported that your son is involved in the black market and is hiding goods in your home!"

"There is nothing here" the woman said, "but you are free to search the house."

As the Nazis went upstairs to investigate, the woman raced to the basement to warn the Altenhaus family.

"You must leave!" she cried.

"Leave! Where will we go?" Isaac exclaimed.

"Anywhere! Just leave! Please!"

Her body was still shaking as she climbed the stairs to the bedrooms on the second floor, hoping to stall the soldiers.

Isaac had no time to think. He pushed his family into the courtyard and with little hesitation guided them into the watercloset. They crowded together in a cohesive knot. Fear gripped their hearts. They died a thousand deaths as they envisioned the photograph of the old grandfather in his skull cap, so foolishly displayed on their dresser.

Upstairs the Nazis had opened the doors to three bedrooms and found nothing. Satisfied with this, they started to leave.

"I wish to use the toilet. Where is it?" a young soldier asked.

"Downstairs in the courtyard," the woman mumbled.

Making his way to the courtyard, the Nazi stopped in front of the watercloset. He was about to open it when he spotted the urinal. In a few minutes, the soldiers left empty-handed.

Frantic with fright, the woman told the Altenhauses that they must leave at once. In driving rain, suitcases in hand, the family began their weary journey back to their home in Antwerp.

Their house had been boarded up since August. It was now late October and the neighbors had given them up for dead. Better this way; anonymity increased their chances of survival. With no heat or electricity, only a kerosene lamp, the family set up housekeeping as best they could. Mrs. Carpentier, their trusted friend and lifeline to the outside world, brought food bought with money that Isaac had saved. But this was not enough and Anneke would sneak through the darkened streets of Antwerp to secretly purchase food from the sympathetic grocer and dairyman. The danger of those excursions was intensified by the nightly street raids which were carried out by the Gestapo.

In their absence, the house next door to the Altenhaus family had been converted into a brothel. On occasion, a Nazi soldier would stumble down the street and mistakenly knock on the Altenhaus door, demanding to be let in. The terrified family would pray that each night would not be their last.

Every day was a struggle to survive. The uncertainty of their destiny created an atmosphere of anxiety and despair. Mrs. Carpentier often brought news of the war's developments that she learned from British Broadcasting Company reports. On a map of Europe and North Africa, Isaac would methodically mark the progress of the war. Strategically planning its end, he gave hope and encouragement to those he loved so dearly.

As the months went by, the money dwindled and hunger set in. Maggots crawled from their mouths as they devoured the spoiled food. No one even noticed. Nothing mattered now. Their hunger was so devastating that there were times when they would drift in and out of consciousness.

When available, herring and sardines were their main staples. Isaac would often humor his family by asking, "Well, my darlings, how would you like your herring today?" With all they had been through, their sense of humor was still intact.

The food situation was a growing concern. There was so little money left, the family decided to send Anneke over to the Zurich home to collect the bolts of cloth left earlier.

"I'm sorry Anneke," Mr. Zurich explained. "Your bolts of cloth were stolen by a house painter we hired some time ago. Now go home, there is nothing you or I can do!"

Mrs. Carpentier was outraged at the Zuriches' dishonesty. With Anneke in hand, she paid the family a visit.

"How dare you treat the Altenhaus family this way!" Mrs. Carpentier cried. "You must give them back their bolts of cloth so they will not starve! If you will not do this," she threatened," I promise that my son who is a police officer, will make it very difficult for your family!"

Anneke and Mrs. Carpentier went back to the Altenhaus home, not realizing that they were being followed by the Zurich family, newly-ordained Nazi collaborators!

A week later, Anneke dreamt the Gestapo came for her family. In her dream she knew that they would never spend another night together.

The next day was Simchat Torah. This special day brought with it a ray of hope. It was a Tuesday in October, 1943 exactly one year since the Altenhaus family came back to their home to live in secrecy.

The family was attending to the holiday preparations, while Anneke agonized over whether or not she should tell her parents about her dream. She didn't want to upset them, especially this day. Despite the fact that she needed someone with whom to share her fears and anxieties, she decided not to mention the dream.

Later that evening there was a banging on the door:

"*Mach auf Juden!* Open up Jews!" boomed a loud and terrifying voice.

Their hearts sank as panic gripped the family. Huddled together, their pulses beating rapidly, adrenaline pumped hot flashes through their bodies. They were trapped! There was no way out this time. Isaac, in shock, proceeded to answer the door.

"Juden!" a Nazi collaborator yelled as he tried to switch on the hall lights. "You stupid Juden! Your lights are out because you do not pay your bills!"

Two storm troopers held Isaac while the collaborator pounced wildly on him, beating him into a bloody pulp.

"No! Please! Do not hurt my Papa! I beg you, please!" Anneke cried, tears streaming down her face.

"Shut up Jude!" screamed the Nazi. "Go upstairs and collect your belongings. You all will be coming with us!"

Anneke, still trembling with fright, managed to walk up the stairs to her bedroom. She grabbed her bed pillow, hugging it tight, as though it was her only friend.

As they shoved the family into the black limousine, Anneke spotted the Zurich family standing on the other side of the street, gloating with satisfaction.

No one said a word as they rode through the blackened streets of Antwerp. The horror stories that they had once heard about were now becoming reality. Ironically, after all those tormenting years of hiding and waiting for their inevitable doom, their capture brought with it a sense of relief. Suddenly the car stopped and a storm trooper dragged Anneke and Mina out. They never saw their parents again.

The orphanage was under the auspices of HIAS (an organization formed to aid displaced Jews). Of the 60 children who stayed there, 16 were war victims waiting to be deported to Auschwitz. Anneke and Mina were part of this group.

The first week Anneke was there, she remained in shock, speaking to no one except Mina. She cried continually, scarcely able to contain her grief. However, the necessity to be strong for Mina's sake overrode her personal needs.

While at the orphanage, Anneke befriended Sonya, a girl her age. They shared their adolescent secrets and fantasies, and each became the family the other no longer had.

In November, the orphanage prepared to close. The group of children who were brought there because of the war were to wait at the orphanage for deportation to Auschwitz. The others were to be taken to the Provence de Brabant, Belgium, where a Jewish sympathizer had offered his chateau to the orphans.

On the day they were to leave, the White Brigade, a division of the Belgian Resistance, destroyed the deportation orders for the 16 children to be deported to Auschwitz. Anneke and Mina joined those moving to Brabant.

The children were lined up by twos waiting for the train to Brabant when suddenly a woman's voice cried out, "Anneke! Anneke Altenhaus! Is that you? What are you doing here, Anneke?"

Anneke looked up and immediately spotted a Gentile friend of her mother's. Embarrassed and humiliated by her now lowly status, Anneke shamefully avoided the woman's eyes and hurried onto the train.

The chateau was run like a kibbutz. The children performed their daily chores under a regimented schedule. They had been there only three weeks when Mina was stricken with scarlet fever and hospitalized. Anneke became hysterical when they took her sister away, thinking she would never see her again. The separation was a terrible strain. Sonya and Mina were all she had left now and she needed her sister desperately. Forty days later, Mina returned to the chateau pale and frightened, but cured.

Gestapo agents came to the chateau searching for children 16 and older to use as forced labor in work camps. Anneke trembled with fear as the Nazi lieutenant jerked the bed covers from her bed and snarled, "How old is this one?"

"She's only 14," the director answered.

"Very well!" he replied and stomped out of the room.

They later left with two other unfortunate children who never returned.

Although the children were provided with food and shelter, they suffered a terrible sense of loss. Their families had been destroyed and their egos crushed, but together they were able to adjust to their circumstances. They were survivors. "Children of the Holocaust."

In July of 1944, the director of the orphanage received a call that the Germans were panicking and picking up all Jewish children for execution. He immediately arranged for the children to be transferred to an institution for handicapped children.

The institution was filthy and it didn't take long for the children to become infested with lice. Anneke pleaded with them to let her keep her long braids.

"If you cut them off," she cried, "my papa will not recognize me when he comes to look for me after the war!" She won her case.

Three weeks later, the Americans invaded France and Belgium. In August of 1944, the Germans retreated. Belgium was liberated!

Within days the orphans made their way back to the chateau. There they found the once elegant home completely vandalized, urine and feces everywhere, a souvenir of enraged Nazi soldiers who were thwarted in their plans to murder children.

In December of 1944, an American G.I. arrived at the orphanage carrying chocolates and oranges, looking for Anneke and Mina. It was their cousin Barney from New York. At Antwerp City Hall, he found their dossier which included their present location. Uncle Oscar had asked him to find the girls and bring them back. Although Anneke still had hopes of finding her parents, she knew it was best if they went; arrangements began.

In the spring of 1945, Lisa, Sonya's mother, who had escaped from Auschwitz at the war's end, now appeared at the orphanage looking for her son and daughter.

"Mama, I want you to meet my friend Anneke Altenhaus!" Sonya exclaimed with pride.

"Anneke," Lisa wept, "I was with your parents in Antwerp waiting for deportation to Auschwitz. At Auschwitz they said, 'those who can work, go left. Those who can't, go right.' Your papa suffered from bronchitis and your mama wanted to be with him. They marched to the right. Anneke darling, those who went to the right were gassed."

Two weeks before they were to leave for America, Anneke was on her way to Antwerp to make the final arrangements for their trip. To her horror, the people who had betrayed her family were standing next to her on the trolley. No one said a word. Their faces turned white at the sight of Anneke who was too numb to cry out. The Zurich family quickly got off and disappeared.

Sonya took the girls to the boat. Anneke felt she was severing her roots because she was leaving her parents behind. Although she was told that they had died, a glimmer of hope still remained in her heart.

The new country was a difficult adjustment. For many years, recurring dreams of being chased by storm troopers through Belgian streets made restful sleep impossible. Finally she understood she was safe in America.

In 1972, Anneke briefly left her husband and four sons to visit Sonya in Belgium. It was as though they were 16 again. Their friendship had lasted 26 years.

Before Anneke's departure, they visited Brussels where a monument was erected in memory of the Jews who had died during the war. Isaac, Pepi and Sonya's father were listed alphabetically.

"My name should have been there," Anneke cried, as guilty tears ran down her cheeks.

"Anneke, don't cry," Sonya whispered. "We were blessed with the gift of 30 years of living."

MEMORIES OF A LOST CHILDHOOD
Stefan Grunwald

By Reba Karp

There are times when Stefan Grunwald's mind refuses to remember. It is during these rare intervals that he is aware that there are pieces of him left over, the ragged edges to his psyche that he has tried to discard.

But they are part of him and won't let go.

He looks back now, and not in any attempt to overlook the past which could take its title from Rimbaud's *Season in Hell,* because for Grunwald it was a "Childhood in Hell."

It wasn't that he didn't have any toys, for they are not necessary for growth; it wasn't that he didn't have enough to eat, for obviously the human body has the capacity to survive on very little; it wasn't that he had no home, for any shelter could be considered a roof over one's head, nor was it the fact that he had no shoes, for he still had two feet.

What seems to bother him the most now, was that he had no dignity. As a cast-off from a society which had gone mad, Stefan was a "Jew boy," and as such wasn't entitled to dignity.

He was born in Berlin in 1933. His father was a psychiatrist, art expert and journalist. The latter would lead him to being tortured for writing anti-Nazi tracts and protecting political activists.

Before the attempted genocide, his family was intellectual and secure. He was named after a friend of his father's, Stefan Zweig, the famed author who committed suicide in Brazil with his wife in 1943. Grunwald attributes it to despair and inability to live in Brazil as the Nazis seemingly began to take over the world: "He was a writer out of order," in a world that had no order.

Grunwald's records show that his flight into his "hell" began in 1934. In order to avoid the Nazi vise which was closing in on all Jews, his parents moved in with his grandmother in Upper Silesia, which at the time was on the Eastern border of Germany. "My grandparents owned the second largest cement factory in Germany. Their name was Loewe, it was my mother's family." When forced to run again, his grandmother Irma Loewe stayed behind to try and liquidate the family's holdings. "She stayed until it was too late." In 1941 she was transported to Buchenwald and his father, the liberal journalist, was condemned to death in absentia.

But Stefan and his parents had elected to run, to enter a race for survival that would take them to Vienna, to Italy and finally a pseudo-haven in Switzerland. But while hopscotching from one torturous experience to another, the one common denominator, beside the hunger and degradation, was the persecution simply because they were Jewish—and this persecution preceded the arrival of the Germans, from whom they managed to stay one step ahead.

From Upper Silesia, Stefan and his mother stopped briefly in Vienna. His father had gone ahead to Italy. They planned to join him later, when he had made preparations for their arrival. But they could not wait for his preparations. In the middle of the night, there was a knock on the door. It was no longer safe for them in Vienna. They would have to leave immediately.

Stefan was only 3, but images from that train ride return. His mother Ruth, who looked Italian, kept speaking Italian to him. He was confused. She was extremely anxious and when any one opened the door to their compartment, she made herself look busy in an effort to conceal her inner turmoil.

In her haste to leave Vienna, she packed what she could. But in her hurry to be reunited with her husband, she left all her belongings on the train. Their search for housing was hampered by the alliance between Germany and Italy which had grown stronger. They settled in the city of Sestri-Levanti, in cramped quarters. Their goal was to eventually cross the border into Switzerland, and to this end, his father Michael made frequent trips back and forth, seeking refuge for his family. Finally, he found lodging for the family in the home of a farmer where they hoped to "sit out the war." But the Swiss closed the border to legal refugees before they could leave.

Boxed in, they remained in Sestri until 1939, when they had to flee once again. This time it was to a refuge in the Italian mountains. But it was only a brief respite, for the Italian farmer who took them in became frightened for his own safety and put them out.

A gray automobile drives out of his past. He can still see it and hear his mother crying. The year was 1940 and the car was driven by the Gestapo who picked up his father and took him to Genoa, where he was questioned about the Italian resistance.

After two days of interrogation and torture, his father returned, only to be taken away again 10 days later. He was released this time at the intervention of a very old Italian family, who had enough ties in Genoa to "put pressure on the Germans."

But there were strings attached to his release this time. The Germans wanted him to spy on the resistance. He had 11 days to make up his mind. His decision was immediate. Once more they fled, literally leaving everything behind.

A former educator (taught at Old Dominion University, Norfolk), Grunwald has a philosophical nature that is stoic yet not severe enough to lack humor, for he distinguishes his life after Sestri as the time "when the bad things began," and perhaps all that came before could be by comparison, considered "good."

As the Germans moved nearer, they were placed in an Italian detention camp outside of Sondrio, where they were lodged in what appeared to be an empty apartment building, with no lights, no heat and no facilities. "We had to drag straw in for sleeping. There was no food, no water, no clothing and no communication with the outside." What food they had was begged from neighboring farmers, but their diet for the most part consisted of bark from trees, which they boiled for tea; and their days were spent foraging for twigs to burn for warmth.

Only the children were permitted outside the compound and this was to beg for food. However, Grunwald remembers that hunger was not his only adversary. Older Italian children thought him easy prey for their pent-up anger and frustrations and caught him and beat upon him.

Begging for food and running from bigger and stronger peers are only torn fragments from his childhood. He witnessed suicides, heart attacks, death by starvation and disease and the weeping and shrieking of those going insane.

"These were people who before had never been in a hostile environment." Aside from the lack of physical necessities, there was the psychological torture of waiting. "The constant threat of being taken across the border to Germany. Some couldn't handle it any longer."

Grunwald dates his "liberation" from the detention camp in the spring of 1942. This, he attributes to his father's friendship with the Mayor of

Milan, who arranged a short stay for them in a cold room above a railroad station. Then they moved to an abandoned apartment building in Colico, with no facilities and no window glass. The family survived on a meager salary his father made by teaching French, Italian and German. To supplement his father's income, "I started stealing."

It was 1942. School was only an illusion, for as soon as he walked into class, the teacher made excuses to send him elsewhere. "She was determined to keep me out of the classroom."

If life was cheap, it was also precious—and he and his parents were reminded of this when German soldiers fired into their apartment. "The Germans only left because they were sure they had killed us. We survived by lying flat on the floor."

It's the psychological factors that stick in the mind, he said, explaining that although they were living in a community, they were totally isolated. By 1943 the Germans were in Colico and as a consequence, the Grunwalds were only permitted to be the living dead. "We had no food and we were living in a town where food was available. The Italians were hypocrites. We were the token Jews. Their intention was starvation. We were given no jobs...their technique was to kill us by starvation." At one time their diet consisted of stray dogs, cats and squirrels.

"I'd get up in the morning, starved. I began the day looking for food. I go to school, come home at noon and still no food; back to school and then back home to no food."

His father joined the resistance and, as a consequence, was told to leave the community. It was early 1943. "The police came to the door and said 'out!' We were not allowed to take anything. We were told to be out of the community in a half hour."

"We wandered the mountain for an hour...we found a cave. We ate chestnuts." Eventually, they joined up with a multi-national band which had formed a mini-resistance, a band of displaced people.

"Now the weapons began to come in...the children stole them from German tanks and trucks." The Germans, at this time, had totally taken over the adjoining countryside. "They went into the best houses, took over the railroad."

The memory of that time is "hunger, hunger and cold. No school and, of course, total chaos." Sleep was frequently interrupted by the warning, "The Germans are coming!" Then it was a mad scramble to get up into the mountains to hide. When the threat subsided, they returned.

"Fear! It took me 50 years not to know fear. I became a person with no personality. I still get upset by the police. I had no peace, there was constant mental anguish. A child needs routine. You eat dogs and cats which is totally against the child. You become ready to lie. Reality and unreality are the same," he said.

Even friendships were illusions in reality. Real before the shot was fired; a fragment from a nightmare afterwards. He remembers just such an incident. He had come down from the mountain with a friend to sabotage a German truck. A round of fire came at them. His friend was hit and fell at his feet as he started to run back up the mountain. More shots, shouts, a spotlight followed him. Two hours later as he lay exhausted, the cry "Germans!" forced him from his fitful sleep to run once more from the Germans. "It was unreal!"

Pressure from the German army increased during July and August of 1943. The refugees were forced to move deeper into the mountains to avoid being captured. "My parents started talking about leaving Italy. Suddenly, there was money for a guide into Switzerland. They spent the night talking. Later the guide was shot. My father had already given him money."

In desperation they persisted. Another guide. Another set of instructions. Grunwald remembers them well. "We walked up the mountain. We were later picked up by an automobile…we weaved in and out of skirmishes with the Germans. We were dropped off at a stable. Down in the valley was a half frozen river, snow was on the ground. At 9:30 in the night the guide signaled us to go down in the valley."

Once in the valley, a German patrol came by and they were forced to jump into the cold river. "Funny, how you remember," he continued. "I can still see the German patrol walking by; I can hear them talk, see their weapons. I can still smell the smoke (from cigarettes) wafting over." When the danger abated, they pulled themselves from the water. But another patrol came by and they were forced once more into the frigid water. "My mother hurt herself and my father was having a kidney attack. The fear now was of being overheard."

Eventually, they reached the barbed wire which separated Italy from Switzerland. The guide handed his father a pair of wire cutters and ran away. They were on their own now and there was no turning back. But there was more to getting through than cutting the wire, for the wires were laden with bells and any attempt to tamper with them would sound the bells and alert the Germans.

His father snipped the wire and they hurriedly crawled under, scratching and scrambling for safety as the now-alerted Germans descended upon them. "We had to climb a steep hill. I have since been back and I don't see how we made it. My father got shot in the leg and my mother tried to pull him up the hill. At that point, the Swiss border guards intervened and helped pull him up. It was an incredible scene."

That was October 3, 1943. On October 6 or 7, the Swiss refused to assist any more escaping refugees. "We had a suitcase of meager belongings and as we scrambled up the hill, it opened up and all the contents fell out. We entered Switzerland with nothing."

His father was taken to a hospital and he and his mother to a schoolhouse. "I was given my first hot chocolate…I can still smell it, feel that cup in my hands. We were given blankets, they were the first in a long time. We didn't see my father for five days. My mother and I were taken to a Swiss reception camp."

But the war was not over for Grunwald. The brief sojourn in the schoolhouse was only the eye of his storm, for afterwards would dawn what he describes as "the worst period of my life as a Jew boy." What made him different? he questioned. He felt like everyone else.

"The underpinning is, you are experiencing being Jewish on the front line! Never has being a Jew come as close to me as then. Young people don't run anymore. After liberation, for 20, 30 years all I did was run. Running in Jewish people is a pathological factor," he said, drawing from Joseph Roth, a Jewish writer. "The difference between fear and anxiety is for fear, you see the danger; anxiety is hidden. All I've been doing for the last 40 years is running."

Shortly after the schoolhouse encounter, his mind rebelled. It simply could not accept anymore cruelty because he was Jewish. "The most astonishing thing happened. I blanked out for three months. The next thing I realized I was in Basel. I don't remember getting there. I was living with a Swiss Christian doctor. He was a sympathizer with the plight of the Jews. My mother and father were put in a Swiss detention camp."

Now, when he rationalizes about the blackout, he feels it was not only related to the anxiety which preceded it, but also to the fact that for the first time in his life, he had been separated from his parents. "I had always been with my mother. Maybe I protected myself by going blank."

It was January 1944. But for a child returning from a long sleep, time was meaningless. "The doctor and his wife had two children who had been killed two months apart, they were about my age. The wife kept their ashes in urns in a semi-darkened room with flowers. Periodically, I was expected to go in and pray. I did that once or twice and then refused."

His punishment. Deprivation once again. "Here I was in a house with everything, but I was deprived. The good doctor was seldom home." Grunwald's days were spent trying to get back into the house, if he was out; or trying to get out, if he was inside.

"The biggest mistake the Swiss made was putting children into homes without first checking them out," he said.

But Grunwald must seek a balance and goes within his memories and finds more pleasant thoughts. Two families had treated him humanely; one was a curator of a museum who eventually procured a job for his father and the other was a Swiss Jewish family.

But a ragged edge of his memories protrudes as he recalls the disorientation he experienced when he had the opportunity to visit his family in the detention camp. His mother was pregnant, there were no facilities and the diet was rudimentary. "It was depressing to be there."

But he was ready for a new home. His stay with the Swiss doctor was over, and his trip from the home of the doctor to the museum director was both physically and psychologically painful. The latter was caused by the badge he was wearing which labeled him, "Juden Kind," which he explains did not carry the same connotations as it did in Nazi Germany. Nevertheless, he tore it off.

The physical discomfort was caused by wearing shoes that were too small, too narrow and with holes in the bottom. "I was in constant agony. I often called these shoes the 'concentration camp for my feet.' I had two choices, either wear the shoes or go barefoot." It was winter and the alternative was just as painful. "I had a pair of socks and it was full of holes."

His stay at the home of Herr Simonett, the museum director in Brugg, was a pleasant respite, but it did not last long as the Swiss families only committed themselves for limited periods.

He was next assigned to a family who had four children of their own, a period labeled, a "living hell." Conditions in their quarters were cramped, and the "mother was an absolute Hitler in terms of her attitude toward children," he said. Little things annoyed her, such as a child neglecting to wash his hands after going to the bathroom. "She would beat the hell out of you," Grunwald said.

It was winter of 1944-1945 and except for his stay with the Simonett family, he had missed the perimeters of even the most limited childhood. It was cold. He had to go to school without warm clothing. "I had to walk to school without decent shoes. I caught pneumonia. They let my father out of the detention camp to visit me. I told him all I wanted was to get to a warm place and stay with him."

At this point, Grunwald had not even seen a doctor. Later his condition grew more severe and he was finally taken to the hospital. Now greatly concerned over his son's well-being, the elder Grunwald was able to get his son removed to another home, this time with a Jewish family, the Haarpuders, an older couple.

It was yet another pleasant respite from a childhood of running, fear and disorder. Then, in 1945 the Grunwalds managed to become a family again, and the three of them and Stefan's new brother Thomas moved into quarters at a hotel. His father was given a temporary job in the museum.

But it was a long time before Grunwald could escape from the limitations of his childhood, for even as his life tried to normalize itself, he was reminded that he was a refugee and "a Jew boy." Among the most painful and persistent incidents throughout his childhood in Switzerland was the taunting by his schoolmates, encouraged by the children of the family whom he had lived with temporarily. Grunwald reasons that this was prompted by the anger they felt, "the certain shame and element of failure" attached to a refugee being removed from their home.

Then, too, until the war ended, they had to endure "The incredible fear and anxiety" of the constant threat of being extradited back to Germany. "You had to get permission to remain from one month to another."

Grunwald lived in Switzerland until 1953 when he came to New York. His father died in Switzerland in 1957; his mother in 1967. He has two brothers living in Switzerland, one a psychologist and the other, a specialist in repairing antique clocks.

Grunwald served in the U.S. Army from 1954 to 1956 and received his Ph.D. from the University of Colorado in 1965. In 1968 he was called to Norfolk by the chairman of Old Dominion University for a visiting professorship and stayed until 1979 when he left for a career as the motivation and force behind Grunwald and Radcliff Publishers.

Today, he puts his life in order as a former academician and as a publisher, for he is now seeking new ways to turn his suppressed anxiety and fears into creativity; to express the positive aspects of being Jewish and to this end, he is focusing on a new publishing venture, Ben-Gurion Books and Educational Materials.

"You can take the bad and it sinks you, or you can make it a force and it takes you up." The Ben-Gurion Books are important to him. It is more than an affirmation of faith; it is an affirmation of Jewish life.

To survive as a child, he had to continually adapt to new environments and in many ways, hostile environments. "In order to survive, you had to lose your personality completely, you became a grand liar, you lived a grand illusion, that it is really not you. You adapt not to be beaten. You sublimate your personality, invent things not there and you begin to believe the grand illusion."

One such illusion, that he had a sister, he carried into his adult life. "It is a fantasy that you have someone else," (who cares) and it becomes so real others are convinced they have seen or met such a person." He recalls being told by an acquaintance that he saw his sister on a New York subway—a woman who existed only in Stefan Grunwald's mind!

Today, he is content with reality, which is greatly intertwined with the survival of Judaism—a faith he once tried to reject, and to that end he bounced from one side to the other of the love/hate spectrum. "At one point or the other you blame Jews. You begin to hate something inside you."

Caring for other Jews is important, for from a "totally screwed up beginning in New York," he was able to put things in order with the help of Lawrence Heller and his family, those he calls "absolute Jews."

"They were the first people who took me in. Shabbat appealed to me. Suddenly I was made to feel like a *mensch*. It was an important factor in my life. I fell from some kind of hell into a Jewish cushion." To his re-emergence as a human being and as a Jew, he also gives credit to his first wife, Harriet Ross.

"From my viewpoint, the Jews of America saved my life." Nightmares are rare now; running away, flights of the past. From the hungry child with no shoes on the cold, cobblestone streets of Italy and Switzerland, he views himself as the emerging *"Yiddisha Mensch,"* one who insists on human rights, dignity and security for himself as well as for other.

To My Baba

*I met you only once; You were
    on flight from Europe to
these shores.
Of the most precious things
    you took along*

were two white pillows
with which you and your
husband
had started many years of
marriage.
Aside from that I knew you not.

However, like echoes from
the past
through your daughter Irma, and
granddaughter Ruth, my mother,
come aspects of yourself
that shaped my life in
many ways:
kindness and empathy;
strength and conviction;
a life centered in family,
friends and children;
good cheer and humor
in times of hardship;
caution in days of brightness.

A tough woman you must
have been,
because your lineage does
reflect that down to me.

All those aspects, no doubt
will make survivors
of my children too.

Baba, Baba, no sweeter
words we have except
perhaps for Mama, mama dear.

—Stefan Grunwald

*My past often grabs me
like a furious pack of
        howling wolves.
Red and Black swastikas;
        the dead eyes of my
        grandmother;
helpless children's exploded
        brains;
the acrid smells of burning
        ovens;
grown-ups in putrid mass
        graves,
pervade my screams—filled
        nightmares,
spilling terror/fear/
        confusion into the every-
day where function I must.*

*Forty-years of childhood—
        youth—adolescence—
manhood, spent running
        from the wolves.
No platform, peace, security.*

*Four decades of painful
        illusions.
And yet, I HAVE SURVIVED
        IT ALL.*

*I've tamed the pack, made
        it docile.
I trained the beasts into
        guardians,
of my heritage around
        the world.
There are many like me.
        Beware Anti-Semite!
Neither touch my children*

nor people.
If ever you do, I'll sic
    my pack
of well-trained ferocity
    on you.
My fellows will unleash
    theirs' too.

We'll overtake you with
    our brains,
sharpened by pain and
    sorrow.
We'd rather smother you
    with culture,
love, and kindness, our
    classic heritage.
But, if that won't do
    we'll sic...

—Stefan Grunwald

FORGED PAPERS AND CHUTZPAH: HER LIFELINE
Dvorah Gutterman

By Reba Karp

Dvorah Gutterman is a small quiet woman. But her gentle outward appearance is in conflict with the turmoil within, for the memories of man's inhumanity to man are her constant companions, memories of atrocities which won't fade and diminish with the passing of time.

"Why?" she questions softly as she begins to recall the years she was forced to live under the sentence of death—from 1939 when war became imminent in Poland until the culmination of World War II in 1945.

Her experiences were uniquely horrible, for she was on the outside, looking into the barbed wires of the concentration camps, living on forged Polish papers which made every Pole her potential enemy. "When the Gestapo would walk by me, they weren't looking me in the face to see if they could detect any signs of my being Jewish. But not so with the Polish people," she said.

Before the war Dvorah lived with her family in a small Polish village of Wislica. "My family was very religious. My father was a Hasid, 'devaning' was the biggest honor to him," she said, explaining that her home was frequently the scene of happy religious activity. On Simchas Torah, the men would march in joyous prayer with the Torahs from the shul to their home where food and merriment awaited them.

Her family was wealthy by the standards of the day, she recalls, dealing in wholesale and retail leather goods. But they shared with those less fortunate.

"My father would lend money without interest," she said, explaining that it was the custom among the village poor to pick up their stipend of money from her father after Shabbat each week. With this money, they would bargain during the week, buying food and paying back other debts. Then on Friday night, just prior to Shabbat, they repayed her father, with the loan cycle resuming again Saturday after Shabbat. The underlying reason behind what appears to be a complicated lending system was basically simplistic—"so the people would not feel they were recipients of charity," she said. (Maimonidies' highest degree of charity—to aid the poor by giving them a loan or job so that they can adequately support themselves.)

Additionally, she recalls with special pride, "pushkas" for many Yeshivas bursting with coins in their home. "My mother knew when someone was sick in the village and would fill containers of food before each meal for those in need. These she would deliver before she sat down for her food."

Another memory, that of an old woman who had been paralyzed and who was forced to live with her impoverished daughter and grandchildren fills her thoughts. "My mother organized the neighbors to feed the woman and to give food to her family. Our day was Wednesday," she said, recalling how she would carry the basket to the family so that all could eat.

She is honored by other and similar memories of her family, rich in Jewish ritual and charity. Then other memories take over and she is forced to question why people so good and pious were allowed to suffer. "It seems so strange," she said. "It is as if I went to sleep surrounded by my large family and when I woke up five years later, there was no one left." (Her oldest brother Pinchas survived Auschwitz and is now living in Australia).

But it was not the sleep of relief. She experienced, rather, the nightmare of five years of the Holocaust.

She dates her personal struggle with the war as occurring on Friday evening, Sept. 1, 1939. At the time she was married and pregnant with her eldest daughter,Sheila and living with her husband in Sosnowiec, where he owned and operated a flour mill. Since they were not far from the German border, by Saturday morning everyone was in a panic..."burning papers and money they didn't want to fall into German hands." Fearful of an immediate attack from the Germans, they fled, with other family members to Wislica, to be with her parents. They tried to reach their destination by train, but the tracks were hemmed in by the approaching war. "For miles and miles, nothing moved. But we couldn't leave the train until daylight at which time we began to walk...we lost contact with some members of the family along the way. There were crowds of people running. We didn't know where we were running."

But sanctuary was not to be found at Wislica, for there they learned that Dvorah's brothers and father had sought refuge in the village of Lublin and followed them, hoping that the extra miles between them and the Germans would offer them relative safety.

But it was not to be. "We never arrived in Lublin, we found out along the way that the Germans were already there and, " her eyes grow misty, "we realized that we couldn't run away. We returned to Wislica."

The journey by foot from Sosnowiec to Wislica and toward Lublin and finally back to Wislica was a trial of survival and endurance. They were frequently without food and water. They slept outside and huddled together in the fields. "Money was worthless," she said. That they survived at all was due to chance encounters with open Polish farms where they found raw potatoes and carrots in the fields. All other food the farmers hoarded for themselves.

After their return from their futile trek toward Lublin, they spent a few days in Wislica, a time of fear and uncertainty. "Although we had mixed feelings and fears, we didn't think there would be gas chambers. But we expected bad times, a very hard future. But we had no choice. There was no way out."

And so the little band of refugees, armed with the indomitable Jewish spirit for survival, decided to return to Sosnowiec and what fate awaited them there. They hired the services of a Polish farmer who took them halfway to their destination and then forced them out of his wagon.

"He threw us out...we had to walk the rest of the way," a journey made more difficult by the presence of her brother's two children. But it was a sad homecoming, for once at Sosnowiec, they found their worst fears realized, for the Germans had put locks on her husband's flour mill and to remove them would have been an immediate death sentence.

"They took everything. But my husband's partner, who had remained behind, had managed to get out a couple of sacks of flour, which were like sacks of gold. We found a baker to make bread and we bartered for other food."

And then they waited—through the uncertainties of the day and the fears of the night—for their unknown future to catch up with them.

It did, in the form of a notice posted several weeks later, that all Jewish men had to report to Gestapo headquarters. Black letters upon white paper spelling death. And so they sought to escape once more.

"The Judenrein were on the watch for those seeking to get out of town." But they had a plan. "I went first, giving prepared signs and signals to my husband and brother when I saw a Judenrein approach," she said.

Around each corner—fear; across each street—the enemy. But to those seeing the young Jewish woman on the street, she was merely on an errand. At times she had to nod to those passing, hoping they could not detect her fearful heartbeat, nor the frightened figures who followed close behind her.

"We made it to the train stop and boarded for Remdcin where the order for Jewish men to report to the Gestapo had not yet been issued," she recalled.

They sat huddled in fear, for it was a train which stopped at stations along the way, during which time a German soldier would board and give the brutal order: "Jews out!"

"We knew about this beforehand and decided we would stay on the train, but the sound of his voice, so thunderous…I didn't just get up, I was picked up by the voice and forced out."

Her fellow travelers through fear experienced the same heat of hate in the soldier's voice and followed close behind. They walked the rest of the way and stayed with relatives in Remdcin until her husband and brother left for Wislica to join her parents once again.

Her destination: the only choice left; she returned to Sosnowiec. "How could I just leave everything? We were hoping that things would calm down and we could start life again."

However, that was not meant to be and as the war closed in on her in 1940, she rejoined her husband. "Life was very difficult, even though we always had enough to eat." Although it was a death sentence to do so, her family was still selling leather goods they had managed to hide before the Germans took everything from them. If the Poles, who bought the merchandise wanted to report them, they would have all been shot. "The Jewish people were not only surrounded by German murderers, but by Polish murderers as well."

She views her life then as a series of knots tied together, each needing the one preceding it in order for it to be tied, and each part of her ragged lifeline to survival. "There was no smartness involved. Things just happened. I never knew what to do, but I had to do something—and it often turned out to be right.

"We lived in a shtetl which had been converted into a ghetto. Cross over the bridge and be shot, unless you had permission from the Gestapo. We lived in fear, subjected to searches and other humiliations."

Resignation, coupled with the Jewish determination to survive, settled in until 1942 when it became apparent that the Germans were systematically liquidating the ghettos. "We knew our days were numbered once again. Fortunately we had planned ahead, for my parents and husband to be hidden underground by a farmer." Since she had had her baby, it would have been virtually impossible for her to join them. "But I didn't look Jewish. It was worth millions. I obtained forged Polish papers through the underground for myself and my baby," and thus she became a woman without an address, past or future, seeking sanctuary and lodging at whatever door fate led her. Many doors opened and many doors closed, and for a short while she lived with a Jewish family in Dcialoseyce until the Germans started liquidating the Jews in the town for a second time.

She fled once more into uncertainties with only the address of a woman in Jedenjuw who might be willing to help her. "I caught a train with my little girl, not knowing where I was going. It was toward the end of September. Winter started very early that year. The train was full. I was standing on the platform between two cars.

"It was cold. I asked permission to get my little girl in the doorway so she would be a little warmer. I was still on the outside. Someone recognized my voice, even in the dark, and threatened to turn me in to the Germans at the next stop. After all, I was Jewish and had no right to live."

The train continued on its journey into the dark. She held onto her child, unable to feel the motion of the train or the emerging winter cold...now only conscious of fear and the desire to live.

She quickly lost herself and her child in the crowd that departed from the train and wisely decided not to go into the train station, even though it would have offered her a buffer against the cold. "I remained outside until another train came. If I had gone into the station and the woman who threatened had seen me, I don't know what would have happened."

When she finally found her way to the house in Jedenjuw, the woman was hesitant about letting her in. Dvorah edged closer to the door, lest it be closed. Where else had she to go? "Miraculously there was another Jewish man hiding in the house and he pulled me in." But her sanctuary was to be short-lived, for she was to remain in the house for only a month before she was told she would have to leave. Forced out among uncaring strangers again, she moved in with another Polish farmer who was in need of money. "The farmer was poor, he sold me a loaf of bread and a bucket of potatoes." This was to last her for the month. "I didn't eat the bread. My baby needed nourishment."

Here, she was fortunate enough to be befriended by the farmer's daughter who taught her Polish expressions, mannerisms and Catholic prayers. "How to behave if I had to go to church to save myself."

The daughter of the farmer was among the more educated Poles and tried to treat Dvorah as a fellow human and even offered her extra food, such as noodles with bacon grease. "I really wanted to eat it," she said. "But I couldn't. I could not eat the grease."

This respite from the outside ended abruptly as the Germans began to take a census among those living on the farms. "The family was afraid and I was told to leave." But the farmer's daughter had made a contribution toward her survival.

Once again she packed her simple belongings, took her child by the hand and stepped out into the fear of the unknown. Since she was left with no other choice, she returned to Jedenjuw and found a room across the street from where the Jewish man, who had originally befriended her, now lived with other Jewish refugees. It was January 1943. The temperature was around 15 degrees below zero and her unheated room had a window with two or three missing panes.

During the day she sought the warmth in the house across the street, with the other Jews waiting for the Gestapo to catch up with them. But at night she had to return to her own room in fear of a German surprise "liquidation" raid on the house. Somehow many of these occurred at night, as if the Germans themselves were ashamed of their actions and sought the anonymity of the dark.

Her room had been rented to her by a Polish doctor, who, subsequently, risked his life to register her in city hall as a Polish woman. Then, armed with her forged Polish papers and "chutzpah" she applied for an apartment as a Polish citizen. "I knew I couldn't stay where I was indefinitely for the neighbors could not help but see me leave the house and each night return to my room. We were living in what had formerly been a Jewish ghetto and was now occupied by other Poles."

She was a woman, alone, in a hostile element. Everyone was her enemy. The Poles sought the Jews out and turned in those the Germans couldn't recognize. Unknown faces in any Polish community aroused suspicion, and those who didn't speak perfect Polish were systematically turned in by their neighbors.

She lived in a vacuum of fear, on guard mentally against her own body, innate gestures which could arouse suspicions: physically alert to signals of danger which would send her seeking another temporary refuge. "I spoke good Polish. I had to give the image of being a Pole." When she ventured out, as she had to in order to buy food and to fulfill her role of a Polish woman living without her husband, she ran the risk of someone recognizing her as being Jewish. Someone from one of her former villages whom she could pass on the street as a stranger.

"When you live in fear, your mind gets more active. The human mind gets strong from fear; it builds resistance to death. But I was convinced that I wouldn't survive. My only prayer was that the bullet would come from behind. I didn't want to go through the mental torture of knowing I was going to be killed."

Nonetheless, survival became the challenge, if only for the benefit of her child. She obtained another apartment with her forged Polish papers and with the help of the American money she was systematically receiving from her parents who were still hiding in an underground shelter on a Polish farm. It was February 1943 and another Jewish woman living on forged Polish papers moved in with her. Her name was Marie, and although she offered Dvorah companionship, she made it more difficult for them to blend in with the Polish society, for she spoke very little Polish and was not familiar with their customs and traditions.

But the pathetic pieces left over from Dvorah's encounters with Polish people began to fit. As a camouflage, she put crucifixes upon her apartment walls and went to church every Sunday, using what she had learned from the Polish farmer's daughter. (Despite the hatred exhibited by the majority of Poles, she feels that every Jew who did survive on forged papers, did so with the help from the righteous Poles). "There was much jealousy from the Poles, for many of the Jews before the war were considered wealthy. There is an old saying among the Polish anti-Semites that 'the streets are Polish; but the buildings are Jewish.' "

She taught her child Catholic prayers and reared her as a Catholic child. "I put a cap tightly on her head to cover her dark curly hair...I went out as little as possible, mainly to church or to buy meager rations...I was pretending I was no different from the others in the neighborhood."

But her mind stretched beyond the day. "I had to think ahead of what would happen to Sheila if I had to run. I couldn't live in such a place with a small child." So, in preparation for another emergency, she rented a room in Kielce. It was not much, for it was located in the area of a former ghetto. Water was running down the walls and those who lived in the area were the "lowest class of Poles."

But in spite of its condition, it was to be a haven later for her and her child.

She feels she is alive today because her parents managed to save some American money which they hid in the attic of their former home. It was later taken out of its hiding place by her brother, who at great risk to himself, returned to the house and bargained with the Polish family living there. In exchange for the money, he told them where the family had hidden some leather goods.

"Of course, they could have killed him and had both," she said.

The transfer of money from Dvorah's parents to her was an elaborate and risky plan, but it worked. At regular intervals, her parents would send her an item of clothing with the farmer. Sewn into the garment would be an American dollar or two, "which by Polish standards was worth a fortune." She would take the American money to a flour miller and exchange it for Polish money on which she and Sheila lived. The miller got part of the money for his help in the transaction and a slip of paper, matching another which she would give to the farmer. This was his receipt and he could turn it into the man at the flour mill who would give him Polish money as preplanned by Dvorah.

The money the farmer brought Dvorah kept her alive; and the money she gave him before he returned to his farm, kept her parents alive. "If the farmer knew they had American money with them, he would have killed my family. It was very complicated and at any step along the way, all could be lost. Every time I went to the miller, I didn't know if I would return."

In thinking back, she rationalizes now that this was another reason that she fought so hard to survive. She was her family's link to survival. "They depended upon me."

There was no laughter in Dvorah's life; only tears and the absence of tears. At times when tears were not enough to release her suffering, she sought to inflict pain upon herself. Such was the case when the farmer brought her the news that her brother was dead. "I tore the skin from my face. Marie had to calm me down. Afterward, I had to stay in the house until my face healed. In order to survive, I had to remain calm," at least for the outside world.

She learned that costly lesson, when in a moment of utter despair over her brother's death, she said "oy vey" out in a public situation. Shortly after the utterance, she saw someone walk quickly back to the house.

It wasn't long before she was visited by two Polish policemen. "I bluffed my way, acted calm. But they still wanted to take away my forged Polish papers," she said, explaining that upon checking on them she would have been exposed as a Jewish woman. After they left, taking her papers with them, she asked help from a former Polish pharmacist who had, himself, recently escaped persecution. He knew of her only as a Polish woman struggling to survive. It was a desperate move—but surely the war would end soon—all she needed was a little more time,

He interceded for her before the police had time to check on the paper's authenticity and after a convincing argument, the papers were returned to her. "He told the police I was a very religious Catholic and since the next day was Easter Sunday, I would need the papers in order to go to church." (The papers were identification when being stopped by Gestapo or the Polish police. No one ventured out without them.)

And once again she was forced to flee. This time back to the woman who had taught her Polish habits. However, she was only allowed to stay there two or three days. But even 48 hours can seem like a lifetime to someone who has nowhere else to go. In desperation she contacted other Jewish people whom she knew were in hiding and asked them for help. One suggested that she take her child and go to a health resort area in the mountains, for it was a region which attracted people from other countries who came seeking physical rejuvenation. He felt the international atmosphere would be conducive toward hiding them.

She walked away, trying to put things in perspective. Her thoughts were racing to keep pace with her pulse. How long had she been running? How much more could her body endure before the pressures of the uncertainties tore it apart?

First things first. She needed to get to the health resort in order to find a room before moving Sheila and the only route was a train from Crakow. She hesitated. It was a dangerous route.

"I had nowhere to spend the night," she said, explaining it was too far to return to the farm and she couldn't go back to her former room. "My papers were stamped Crakow, anyone asking to see them would be suspicious of my spending the night in the train station."

However, fate intervened and a Polish official in charge of vacant army barracks, noticing her plight and yet unconcerned about her identity papers, offered her a night's lodging in the empty barracks not far from the station.

She accepted and followed him, fearing that every step would be her last. When she was alone, every sound became her enemy. She did not sleep. It was a long night.

In the morning she caught her train and when she arrived at her destination, everything was closed. It was as a resort area out-of-season. "My mind was racing. I had made the trip for nothing." Once again, the familiar problem. "Where could I spend the night?"

She took a chance and approached a house. A young woman with a child answered the door. "I told her a story, about looking for a place to live with my sick child and that I needed a place to spend the evening. I was a good actress. I played with and hugged her child. I later put the child to sleep and helped her say her prayers.

"The woman offered me a place to stay with Sheila. I told her I would be back. But I didn't return. I was afraid to be so far from my parents. I had the feeling I had to keep my family under my wing."

She had a lot to think about on her return trip to Crakow. How much further had she to travel before she could find peace? At the Jedrzejow train station she saw the same policeman who had visited her apartment and took away her identification papers earlier. Instinct dictated that she avoid another encounter. "I pressed myself up against the wall until he left and I stayed that way. I didn't know when he would return and I didn't know what to expect."

All was not lost, however. She still had her ace; the room she had rented months before in the ghetto in Kielce. When they arrived, even its impoverished conditions seemed as a haven for the three refugees. They were off the streets. "I tried to improvise some furnishings—crosses, Jesus and Mary. I turned a tub upside down for a table, put a blanket over a board to make it look like a bed. We slept on the floor." It would have been dangerous for the neighbors to think they arrived with nothing—it could only mean they were running away from something.

So they settled in their room of fear, waiting for the knock on the door, the gun in the face, until another harmless incident made her vulnerable to German hostilities once more.

"Sheila was playing with some children. They asked her if she was Jewish. The child didn't even understand what was being asked and replied, 'yes'."

It wasn't long afterward that she was visited by two Polish policemen. She tried to play her part again, but this time they were more clever and interrogated her and Marie in separate rooms and then compared notes.

Discrepancies were obvious.

Then, what must have been a preplanned scenario unfolded. Dvorah and Marie were not the only ones playing roles. One left, on the obvious pretense of getting cigarettes, and the other allowed himself to be "hurriedly" bribed.

"We had to flee again. But where? I had no other place to go. Where could you run with a young child?"

The only option left was to put Sheila in a Catholic Children's Home, an involved and dangerous process. "It was an unbelievable task." It required permission from the Gestapo, permission she dared not ask for. And, so once again she fabricated a story. Her husband was a German war prisoner and she had to work in order to support herself and the child, and in order to work, she needed someone to take care of her child.

She visited many children's homes during the next few days and remembers that her feet were swollen from walking. But the response was always the same. She had to have permission from the Gestapo.

"But I continued to look until I found a small home which had only about 100 to 150 children. I told them my story, but with some additions, part of which was that my husband's family lived in Crakow and would probably take us in, but that I had to go there to talk with them first.

"I told the nun that I was starving. I cried, I spent a long time talking to her, and when I finished she told me that she didn't have the strength to tell me 'no,' that she would take my daughter without the Gestapo's permission, even though they would kill her on the spot if they found out."

But the nun made the agreement conditional. "It was temporary. I had to take her out in about eight days."

Aside from the obvious danger of asking the Gestapo's permission, putting her child in a home would have surely meant she would have been deported to Germany to work, she said.

She arrived at the home as planned, with Sheila's personal belongings in one hand and the child, in a new dress, holding on to the other. Sheila was then 3 years old.

Her heart was heavy, for leaving a child crying and begging not to be left, was difficult. But she had no other choice. Still bargaining for time, she returned to the home around a month later and told another story, that her husband's family was too poor to take them in. "I kept thinking that if I had a little more time, the war would soon be over."

At night, as she lay in fear awaiting the knock on her door, her thoughts were with the child she had to leave. She thought of the poor conditions, the lack of food. Sheila's diet at the home consisted of a thin slice of bread and a cup of black coffee in the morning. The main meal was cabbage with water, and again for the evening fare, Sheila got another thin slice of bread and cup of black coffee.

She visited her—when she dared. "One day I found her sick, weak, with sores all over her body. I went out, with great risk, and bought her butter and eggs...I aroused suspicion and was asked to take Sheila out of the home.

"I begged for a couple more days."

At this time Dvorah had managed to find a place for herself, by being the outside connection for other Jewish people hiding in a chimney on a Polish farm. She threatened to leave them without that "connection" unless they helped her find a place for her child. "I didn't know what I was going to do," she remembered.

By chance, one of the Jewish men had had some business dealings with the priest before the war. "He wrote to the priest, told him I was a Jewish woman who had married a Catholic before the war and had converted, that the child had been born Catholic. He told the priest that my husband was a prisoner and the child had been asked to leave the home due to overcrowded conditions. He told him we would both die of hunger if this was allowed to happen."

The letter ended with the man begging the priest to go to the home and intercede for her child. When the letter was finished, Dvorah was once again entrusted with a dangerous mission. She delivered the letter to the priest in person and had he so desired, he could have turned them all in to the Gestapo.

But he chose to help them and spoke to the nuns about the child. But again, the conditions were limited. She was to take Sheila out of the home in a month. This time, however, Dvorah felt a little more at ease with the limitations, for she knew that since the priest had requested asylum for the child, that even if she did not return for her in the specified time, no harm would come to her.

"I didn't see Sheila after that, until we were liberated."

Living in fear for so long had made Dvorah strong, but she had to be in order to make the decisions that she did and in order to take the chances that she dared. One such incident involved her "night in jail," which was a result of her being picked up after being caught sleeping in the back of a wagon. This was during the interval when Sheila was in the home and she could not return to her room after "bribing" the Polish policemen. She had not yet moved in as the outside connection with those hiding on the farm.

Her crime was not so much that she spent a night in a wagon, but the suspicion that she was Jewish. After being forced to endure interrogation with the Gestapo, who "ruled" that she did not "look" Jewish, she was nonetheless put in a Polish jail with other women for the night. It was an evening of mental torture and hell. Her "cell" mates were hardened Polish women off the streets, who, suspecting she was Jewish, subjected her to the most inhumane mental abuse.

In the morning when she was subsequently released, she made the decision to return to the jail on the pretense of picking up a package she had left. Her real motive was to see the women once more.

She picked up her package and looked into the cell at the women who were still locked up. When she was certain that all had seen her, a free woman, she said "goodbye," turned and left the jail. "I had to show them I was alive. This was worth a risk to my life."

Shortly thereafter she moved into her final hiding place and awaited liberation. A long anticipated incident which didn't live up to its expectations.

Upon seeking out her mother and father, she found only an empty underground excavation. "Six months earlier I would have still had my parents; six months later I wouldn't be here," she said, explaining that when she was liberated her arms and legs were covered with blood blisters from not eating, a habit she didn't particularly miss at that point.

Today, Dvorah, a widow, lives in Virginia. In addition to Sheila, she has three other children by her second husband, two daughters and a son who is a physician. Her first husband did not survive the Holocaust.

When asked if she still has faith, she responded during the last interview by referring to an article on "Kristallnacht," which ends with her answer, supplied by the philosopher Emil Fackenheim, who notes that if the contemporary Jew turns his back on his faith, denies that which his ancestor voluntarily died for, then…"Hitler will have won this war from the grave."

"PEOPLE...WERE JUST WAITING TO DIE"
Ruth Igdal

By Reba Karp

On June 21, 1941 Ruth Igdal left her home in Pokrojus, Lithuania to start a new job in Kovno, Lithuania. "I took the train Saturday evening, after Sabbath." It was a beautiful day, she said, perfect in every way to start a trip which would take her 400 miles from her native city. "It was a beautiful little city. My sister Anna had left six months before, I was going to join her. It was an easy feeling for me.

"Friends came to say goodbye. There was much laughter and crying," Ruth added, explaining that living in a small town had limited her possibilities of a job as a bookkeeper, as the Russians, who occupied the Baltic states at that time, gave the jobs to the poorer people.

Ruth adds that, at the time, she did not feel threatened, despite the fact that the area was full of Jewish refugees fleeing from Hitler's advancing German troops. "The Jewish families took them in and gave them room and food. We loved them like brothers and sisters."

Ruth remembers she traveled through the night with other Jewish young men and women. It was a festive time. Not even her worst nightmares gave any indication of what lay before her.

She arrived in Kovno around 8 o'clock in the morning. Her sister and a friend Rita Sands, also a survivor and now living in Philadelphia, met her at the station. Their happy reunion was marred by the confusion of a town under siege. "I thought it was war maneuvers," she said. But the radio, when she arrived at her sister's apartment, broadcast the news that the Germans had crossed the border to Lithuania and that war had been declared between Russia and Germany.

As people in time of trial tend to do, they began to congregate and talk of the pending disaster and the options. "I wanted to go home, but there was no way to get home," she said. But when the radio announced that for every Lithuanian killed, 100 Jews would be murdered, they realized they were in danger.

"We planned to cross the border to Russia, 300 miles away." They packed what they could carry and set out on foot—a small group of Jews fearful for their lives—lost among the thousands that filled the roads as the air thundered with gunfire and the sky filled with fighter planes. After 10 days on the march, buying food from neighboring farms and sleeping where they could find shelter, they realized there was nowhere to go. The Germans had moved in around them.

Once more they huddled together and discussed their options. There was no other alternative but to return to Kovno. "It was a hard journey back," she explained, made all the more uncomfortable for the weary foot-travelers by the Lithuanians, who were now denying them food. What they did manage to get, they shared equally among themselves.

"It was terrible," Ruth continued. "There is no way to explain it." The trip to nowhere which had taken them 10 days, took 14 days to return them to their uncertain fate. "Our shoes were taken away from us. We walked barefoot. We were getting weak. We didn't sleep at night. We cried, talked. We didn't understand what was happening.

"The roads were full of refugees. We had to step over dead bodies, those of men, women and children."

They returned to her sister's apartment, which looked like an oasis after their weary, futile journey. But it was only the eye of the storm. "Jewish people couldn't go out on the streets. There was killing, looting. We were scared to open the door." When, out of necessity they ventured out to get food, they were consistently pushed back to the end of the lines, physically abused.

"The Jewish men were scared to go out because they were picked up and carried away. We women took turns standing in the lines."

"One Sunday morning, my friend Soshana and I went to stand in line. We were identified as being Jewish and were picked up." They were among hundreds who were pushed into another crowd and herded into a school already crowded with Jewish people. From that building they were taken to the "7th Fort," also crowded with frightened Jewish people.

Then the systematic killing of people began. "One woman screamed to go home to her baby who she had left alone. The more the people screamed, the more they were tortured," she said.

"We huddled together, planning to escape when it was dark…many were already dead, many were pretending to be dead. So Soshana and I pretended to be dead."

Ruth lay still among the dying and dead. "I reached out and grabbed Soshana and urged her to run.

"But she said, 'Where?'"

It didn't matter where. Fear had become their ally and urged them on. Little by little they worked their way through the woods until they were once again on the road. And they continued to run, jumping into roadside ditches with the approach of passing cars.

"When we finally made it back to the apartment, we were told we were thought dead. So many had been shot." Later, when there was no food in the city, they ventured out cautiously, pretending to be Lithuanians. "If you got away with it, you got food."

And so they existed until the end of July when it was announced that all Jews had to move into the Ghetto Slabotka. "It was once a shtetl of middle-class Jews. We had until Aug. 15 to move in. The ghetto was closed the next day. No one could come in and no one could go out."

Jewish committees were formed, these were the governing bodies who distributed the food, kept order. Ruth remembers the food—"horse meat, rotten potatoes." Although the inside of the ghetto was overcrowded, makeshift and barely livable, it at least, offered refuge against the hostile world waiting to annihilate them on the outside.

The first "call" was for lawyers and doctors. "These never returned. We were unaware of concentration camps. Then another group. It didn't return either," she added.

"Those young enough had to work. The Germans asked for specific laborers at the gate. These did manage to return after working all day," she said, explaining that in order for those not on work detail to survive, they had to sneak out with the laborers and come back in with the laborers. When the laborers were herded off to work, the others took different routes in search of food.

They learned to survive, to become invisible when necessary. They knew which groups were destined not to return and before the "call-up" they would hide in attics and basements "with the rats."

She remembers much and her thoughts overlap. Other unwanted memories surface. "The Germans locked the door to the hospital in the ghetto and burned it down with the eight doctors, 15 nurses and 45 patients inside. They blamed it on typhus.

"The ghetto was divided into large and small divisions. The small ghetto was liquidated in one week. They were taken to the fort and killed.

"On Oct. 28, 1941 everyone, except the sick, were lined up and told to march between lines of SS officers...one group told to go to the left, one to the right...families were deliberately split...ten thousand were taken to the now empty small ghetto. On Oct. 29 they were taken to the fort and instantly killed...just a mountain of bodies...some still alive and struggling to get away from the dead."

Feelings and emotions were all but extinguished, but not hope. "We had a hope, maybe some of the Jewish people would survive, many felt they would be the one to tell the story." And so they held on even as the ghetto was systematically liquidated. They slept where they found themselves, five and six in a room, unheated. "It was so cold, we would tear the buildings down for wood."

By November 1943 those still alive were taken outside the Ghetto to a camp, "another step toward total liquidation," she said. The camp consisted of barracks with three-tiered wooden planks for beds. Work detail began at six in the morning, ended at eight in the night. The children, old and sick stayed behind.

On March 27, 1944 when the workers returned to camp, they discovered that the old and children had been taken away and killed. "The parents began shrieking. A few children survived by hiding. In anguish the parents wanted to burn the barracks and everyone throw themselves into the flames. But, of course, after the hysteria subsided, they couldn't do it," she added.

"But in the end, they got everyone in some filthy corner to die. I remember as a young woman I had long beautiful hair. It was now full of lice and had to be cut.

"I cried...we were human beings." Had that fact been overlooked by part of the world? she questioned.

Before they were moved once again, from Gifangen Lager Alextos, Ruth recalls that one of her friends escaped from the group and crept back into the now surfacely deserted ghetto. However, beneath the ground Jewish life scurried for existence. Bunkers were full of humanity trying hard to survive by eluding the Nazi vise which was closing in on them.

Here, again, the German murder machine was thorough. The solution was so simple. They bombed the underground shelters with everyone inside. No one escaped.

From the Gifangen Lager, Ruth and her sister Anna were moved to Poneves, where they became a part of a group of Jewish laborers building an airport. Conditions were barbaric. They were beaten with systematic regularity, forced to work hard, fed little and left to sleep out in the open, or if possible in nearby barns, which served to keep them in, more than the elements out.

Two months later, Ruth and her group were transported once again. This time to Shaulen, which was only 35 miles from her home. But all she could do was look over the horizon in the direction of where she spent her last happy moments. Home was so far away. Shaulen was a liquidated ghetto and except for the unquieted spirits of people deprived of their right to exist, all that remained were the lice, roaches and rats, which she said, "grew bigger and bigger each day."

The dehumanizing conditions were overbearing. What remained of her sensibilities recoiled from filth. She sacrificed her ration, of what was considered coffee, so that she could attempt to wash her hair. The dark residue was not so much an attempt to cleanse the hair as to ease the itching. Ruth cries and must stop. The memory of those conditions intrude upon her security even now.

The next stop was Germany, but as Ruth explains, "it was not so quick." Destination unknown, they were loaded into coal wagons, with the men separated from the women—50 people into a wagon. The train stopped abruptly at the Lithuanian town of Tawrig. They huddled together, no longer able to comprehend fear even as the locks to their coal car were opened. The women were told to get out. "But, we had not anything to fear from anyone," she said, explaining that even death would have been anticlimactical. "We were taken to a very big room, it must have been a former store front. We were told to take off our clothes...hundreds of Lithuanians surrounded the window front and peered in at us. Then we were told to dress again. We were not ashamed. We were just like animals.

"But to this day, I still don't know why we were asked to do such a thing."

Later, they learned their destination was Stutthof. They arrived late at night. It seemed so dark. Once more they were carted off as less than human from one group of cars and forced into others..."how much they beat upon us. It was impossible to think of what they would do next," she said.

"I can still hear the noise of a train as it stops...only it is a thousand times worse." Once more she and her sister were behind barbed wire. She looked around her. There were thousands. "We looked from left to right. We couldn't believe what we saw." Now, she rationalizes that Stutthof must have been the last stop for Jews from many different localities. These were the stalwart who had survived only to be waiting extermination.

The systematic separation of families began. The boys who had been isolated with their fathers were now torn away. "They begged to go with their fathers, they promised to do anything, if only they could go with them." Their pleas fell on deaf ears.

Even though the war was winding down, the Germans were still concerned with collecting valuables from the Jewish people. On the guise of delousing the women and giving them showers, they were told to remove their clothes, drop all their personal belongings and move forward into a large room. Before entering they were asked to lift their arms in the air. At first Ruth thought this was part of the delousing procedure. But, when she entered the large room and was forced upon a table for an internal examination in an attempt to remove valuables hidden inside her body, she knew it was only another Teutonic ritual—barbaric and brutal. Afterward she looked out of the back door, and what at first appeared to be a huge mountain, upon closer examination was seen as a huge pile of shoes—all that remained of those who had taken the shower of death.

Since she had nothing more to give the Germans, she was allowed to leave. The women formed a line and were issued makeshift shoes, a dress and a coat. "There was no concern as to fit...after the clothes we were told to run...we were taken to another barracks where we slept on planks piled four layers high...later we traded clothes with one another for a better fit."

For two days they lay upon planks, with no food or contact with the outside world. On the third day, the barracks were opened and the women were told to line up. Ruth remembers there were blocks and blocks of women. "And we stood the whole day in the sun." Just by digging in the sand with their feet they unearthed papers, photographs and other items of those who had stood earlier where they were now standing.

On the fourth day it was a repeat of the same, only they were given a little bowl with what was identified as food, but it looked like long pieces of grass. "Still to this day I don't know what it was." Later she was to pass a barrack which was identified as the hospital. "We saw two people carry out bodies, just sticks with head and feet. Then we knew what it was we had survived for."

The routine became monotonous. "People were just drying up...we were just waiting to die. We lost continuity of the days...we thought even the birds are afraid to come here...the only view was the sand and the sun."

In August of 1944 there was a call for women to work. Everyone was anxious, it was a chance to get out, she said. However, since there were so many women it took a few days until they could even get to her and her sister.

Her new station was Stainort, which she said was considered part of Stutthof.

"We got up with the light and stood in lines for count and then went to work...digging trenches for soldiers...we didn't have the strength to get past the sand...we had picks to break rocks. At noon we were given a bit of oatmeal and a thin slice of bread. We stayed in the heat and worked until dark. We slept in a tar paper hut-like enclosure...on straw. It was impossible to stand up...we had to sleep 50 women, close to one another, there was no space."

The morning revealed those who had died in the night or who were dying. "They were gone by nightfall, when we returned," she said.

In December of 1944 she was in another work camp, in Rewodzik, which offered the same conditions. "The beatings...the madness," she said, recalling the woman who was shot in the head because she ran to get the potato she saw while working in the field.

Then on Jan. 19, 1945 they were awakened earlier than usual. "We heard planes...the Germans were nervous, upset, the whole camp was taken out...we had to walk in the snow...those who turned their heads to look back, were shot." One was her sister-in-law, Sofia Igdalsky.

By night they had reached a village deserted by the Germans fleeing west from the Russians. Ruth and her sister plus four other women huddled in the top of a barn under straw for warmth. "The next day we knew we couldn't go on any further. We hid in the hay...the rest were carried away. We stayed there for three and a half days with no food...we survived on icicles hanging from the roof."

At the end of the fourth day a group of Germans started to establish headquarters in the barn. The women could hear their voices from the loft and realized it would be only a few moments before they were detected.

"We were so weak we hardly looked at one another. But the Germans left suddenly. Then on the sixth day one of the women said she thought she heard a Russian song." The Russians were moving into the area. The date—Jan. 25, 1945.

The group was lead by a Jewish general who offered them help. "We couldn't eat, we weighed only 65 to 70 pounds each...he rubbed our feet with cream...he took care of us for one week."

But their travail was not over. The first group of Russians were replaced by another group of Russians, these looking for women. So the six women fled and hid in the enclosure where the pigs and chickens were kept. "In the morning we looked out the window and saw they too were gone, so we went back into the house."

Finally they were transported by another group of soldiers to Grodna, Poland and moved in with other Jews who had come out of hiding.

"We wanted to go home...we had to register. We stood in line, but as we stood, some people who knew one of the women warned us in Yiddish, that if we stood in line we would be transported to Russia, to hard labor"

They were advised where to hide and were later taken to Jewish homes, where they obtained false passports to send them further west. "We were not to talk on the train, we had to hide the fact that we were refugees," she said. As prearranged at Bialystock they were recognized by the way they were dressed and picked up by other Jewish people who helped them on their way. "We celebrated the first Passover since the war in Lublin...we felt those who met us...everybody was my sister and brother."

Since Ruth and her sister couldn't get to Israel because of Ruth's health, they became part of a network called the Brecha, an organization whose aim it was to help Jewish refugees. Then Ruth became ill from the pus which had settled in her shoulder from continual beatings. "I was told I wouldn't survive unless they amputated the arm."

But the third operation proved the diagnosis incorrect, and while she was recuperating in the hospital her sister, Anna, (now Anna Burk of Virginia) came with the news that Ruth's husband Irving was still alive. Ruth had married him earlier in the ghetto as a matter of convenience to elude early transportation. But it was just a paper wedding, she explained. The marriage of convenience was Oct. 23, 1942. Their formal Jewish marriage was on Dec. 10, 1945.

"I hadn't seen him since Stutthof where someone remembers him hollering behind barbed wire as we were led off, 'Wait for me'."

The Igdals lived in Munich until they moved to America in 1949.

While recuperating in the hospital, she remembered her Aunt Mary Leibman's address in Boston, as it was when her mother had corresponded with her before the war. She gave a letter to an American soldier who sent it through the Red Cross. "When my aunt got the letter she called my sister, Edith Klavans, who was living in Norfolk. Edith arrived in America on the last boat in 1939."

Ruth's lost family is ever on her mind. Perhaps, it is because they disappeared so quickly. "While in the Kovno Ghetto we hoped that our family...had survived by escaping to the Russian border. We prayed for them."

This hope was dispelled by a Gentile woman who had been married to a Jewish lawyer in Pokrojus. He was murdered by the Germans. Through her eyes, Ruth heard the story of how her family and other members of the community were killed.

"The Germans and Lithuanian hooligans...worked together. They ordered all the Jews from their homes, to line up with little food and water. And nothing else. They panicked...children crying and screaming...people asking, 'what is our sin? what have we done? Please God help, help...' God turned them down...

"But I still believe in God. I still do...(even) under beatings with wooden sticks and guns."

The woman told Ruth that her family and the other Jews of the city, were forced to stand for seven days without food and water, dying in the street.

"On the eighth day they forced them at gunpoint to walk three kilometers to the forest at Morkekalve, to dig their own graves...to put boards over the graves and to walk on them...

"Then the Germans and the hooligans started to shoot...the children they threw into the grave alive."

Despite the pain of the Holocaust, Ruth has happier memories, which she cherishes. She remembers her father, Moshe Shapiro who died at 39. "He was a gentle man...he believed in the goodness of humanity. The happiest hours were spent Friday night with the family after shul...the beauty of the Sabbath (in Pokrojus) I will never forget."

Today Ruth and her husband are retired. They have one child, a daughter, Frieda Marlene Igdal, who is a pharmacist.

THE BROKEN HOUR

By Sonia Kogan

If You Were My Friend...

If you were my friend and were to ask me: "Tell me something about the past"...then I would come and sit close by you, put my head on your shoulders and start crying softly, and hesitatingly I would then say: "Once—upon—a time..."

If you were a doctor, a psychiatrist and you were to ask me: "Please, tell me something about the past"...then I would say..."Doctor, I am hurt, here inside," and I would point to my heart, and try to convince him that it is a wound. "I have a wound which constantly aches, Doctor," I would say...

But...you are not my friend and not the doctor, and if YOU should ask me: "Please, tell me something about the past"...then I would say..."shall I tell you a fairy tale? My fairy tale, intended for grown-ups and I would begin with...Once...upon...a time..."

In the house of my childhood there lived a happy family, loving each other deeply with an unlimited love. You could already feel that upon opening the front door. Usually you would smell the flavor of delicious food, and my grandmother, whom I called "Babbe", would stand there waiting for me, smiling and wiping her hands on her apron.

Like the sideboard in the dining room she was always at home. I would run toward her, push my nose against her soft stomach and sniff the smell of the many dishes which were mixed in her apron, together with the smell of her old body. The small, rough hand would caress my hair and cheeks, and usually she asked in Yiddish: "Sonjele, are you hungry?"

She was a short fat woman, illiterate, but with her deep-brown, lively eyes she understood life so wonderfully well. She was a very pious woman, my "Babbe". But her children didn't follow her. They had thoroughly different ideas, different desires...Take my Uncle Jack, of the extreme left;

Uncle Maurits, Aunt Fanny and Chassie, who were expelled from their country in 1930 because they were Trotskyites...

Take Aunt Clara and mother, no political notions, just ordinary domestic drudges...Take father, a fatalist, and Uncle Albert, a French-speaking bourgeois, and the poor little lamb, Eva, who was a living proof of the fervent love between her parents, Aunt Clara and Uncle Albert; this tiny morsel of flesh too became—smoke! What remained most clearly in my mind was the togetherness of the family.

In spite of their widely diverging ideas, in spite of the quick-tempered discussions and differences of opinion, they were one. One-big-square-block-together. When I was sitting in my little corner observing them, I saw their eyes through the flow of words and out of those eyes was shining a deep affection, an immeasurable love...It is through that overwhelming feeling that all the children went the same way as Babbe did. Their very last journey was to the crematorium. Aunt Clara was holding little Eva tightly pressed in her arms, when she was gassed. Later they were found by acquaintances in that position and laid to their last rest, somewhere in strange soil. Not one of the many children had deserted Babbe, who was old and in weak health and who could not possibly travel. Sometimes, I heard father speak in an excited manner: "We have to flee. We can escape to England"—he always said—"across the sea. We've got enough money to start from scratch there." Then as always came mother's answer: "What about Babbe?" That brought every discussion, every conversation about leaving to an end. All attempts to save themselves from Hitler's claws were in each conversation terminated with Babbe. And so it was with the other children. They stayed and challenged death unknowingly!

1 May 1940

On 1 May 1940 I became 10 years old. It was a beautiful evening in spring and there was a feast that lasted all night. But really it was the children's party that made a greater impression on me. I received a gold watch and papa sang in a very sentimental way "Sonny Boy". Ten days later the war broke out. It wasn't really such a big surprise.

Sgt. Uncle Albert had been called up months before and sometimes father said, "There'll be war, it's in the air." To which Babbe replied: "Whatever will be, will be." The Germans were advancing and, like many friends, my parents, too, thought of leaving. England, it would be safe there! In myself I prayed hundreds of times: "Dear God, let it be war." I thought war was just a game, which I played so often with the children in the street. Big fat Aimé, our district policeman's son, was always the commander and, of course, I was the head nurse. I found playing war was an exciting game. My hospital was situated on our sidewalk, where I applied dozens of bandages to the many wounded in the battle. They arrived, dragged on in a wooden box and then I said haughtily, "Lay him down carefully soldier, I will take care of him immediately." Most of the times I first disinfected the leg or the arm with water, which I always had close by me in a little jar.

A few months later father, mother, Babbe, my little brother and I fled to France. We left in a chock-full train. Through the window we waved to the people who were seeing us off…After many hours of travelling we passed the frontier.

I remember how there Babbe, my brother and I were put on a truck, destination Saint-Omer. Because there was not enough room my parents had to travel by other means. We would meet each other at the station of Saint-Omer. Who could foresee what would happen? After a while, the driver forced us to get out. There we stood, the three of us, on a lonely road without any money, food or clothes and my old Babbe who could not speak a single word of French. In the distance we heard some shooting and having walked for a while we saw a motor-road on which many people with carts and all sorts of vehicles were also trying to escape. We were just going to join them, when we suddenly heard a squadron of airplanes.

It caused a deafening noise and all at once they began firing at the many people in our vicinity. We were watching as if hypnotized. As if stunned Babbe said, "Lie down!"

We were lying by the wayside in the fragrant grass. All at once I forgot the dead, because close to me a tom cat and his mate were playing the game of love. After a little while, we set off again and I remember the deserted village with so many dead bodies of soldiers in the streets. There stood a large white farm with dark green shutters. At a certain moment I looked up and saw a soldier hanging out of the window. His head had fallen aside and from his large gaping mouth blood dripped, which left a red mark on the white front of the house…Babbe knelt down near a moaning soldier. He was lying against a wall and looked entirely yellow. From his mouth came jerkily the words, "femme, Lilly, Lilly," I heard. For a long time we have been sitting there on the ground by the soldier and he could still say, "Maman, maman" to Babbe, who had by then taken his head in her hands.

Babbe was crying all the time as if it were her son who was dying there. I had never seen death from that close. Suddenly, the war was horrible. I wanted the safe familiarity of our home and the objects I both knew and loved. Why were all these people suddenly dead? They seemed so young, much younger even than father, who wasn't even 30. And then those strange fixed eyes.

There was nothing but blood, dust, sun and silence. We were thirsty and hungry and in the dead village there was not a living soul who could give us something. "Shall we also die, Babbe?" I asked anxiously.

We did not die. After some time we passed through a burning town, Dunkirk. I saw houses collapse on top of a group of women who were queueing at a shop. I saw little children with bleeding bodies and torn-off limbs, lying on the grey dusty ground.

I looked into a pram where a baby was crowing with clenched fists—his mother was lying beside the sidewalk, killed by a bullet.

The only thing which really hurt was hunger. We knocked at doors and Babbe made a movement with her hand so that they could see that we were hungry. Sometimes we got a chunk of bread and some water. But hunger was the only real feeling we knew in those days. One night we were lying in a cellar with other fugitives, sleeping on the stone floor. I woke up early in the morning and I clearly remember how a feeling of sheer panic struck me and I begged Babbe to get out of the house quickly. "Babbe," I said, "something terrible is going to happen. We have to leave here. We have to get out of here, please Babbe, hurry…"

My Babbe was a very superstitious woman and in my fear she saw a warning sign from God. We left the house and finally returned to the same spot about noon. The house had disappeared, as well as half of the street. The bombardments we had heard in the distance were the cause of all this. When Babbe saw those ruins, she did as I had seen her do many times before. She knelt and thanked God for our rescue.

Babbe remained there for a long time. People came and stood around us and I felt ashamed because that pious Babbe was saying her prayers in Hebrew as if she had forgotten the whole world.

While we were marching further toward Saint-Omer (the only word Babbe kept asking passers-by), I heard her talk to all the dead. She beseeched God that this horror might end soon and that we, the children, might safely arrive at our destination.

"Take my life God," she murmured, "let me die and save these little children, who are still at the beginning of their lives." She held long conversations with God, promised everything. But her prayers always ended with the wish that we might live. She did not speak to us unless it was absolutely necessary. We went through many villages and fields and during a big bombardment we finally arrived at Saint-Omer. Many days had passed since we had left my parents. We were exhausted and entered an empty farmhouse.

I remember the white tablecloth and the vividly colored cushions in the chairs, the flowered curtains and the many bottles of wine that were standing on the sideboard. On the table were plates with leftovers and my brother and I ate them. Babbe was so exhausted that she had fallen asleep. Suddenly, we heard a bumping noise. The family came out of the cellar. They were surprised to see us sitting there, eating those leftovers. From their gestures I understood they wanted to give us some other food. Compassionately, they looked at Babbe, who had meanwhile awakened. With hand-signs she communicated our experiences to them. We stayed for a few more days on the farm with these friendly and hospitable people. Then we went on in the direction of Saint-Omer station.

I remember quite clearly how we went up a rather steep hill; on both sides there were small houses. All of a sudden we saw father and mother coming toward us, it was as if we saw an hallucination. They couldn't believe their eyes either and they ran towards us and their cries and outbursts of joy made the people come out of their houses. We were embraced, Babbe and mother fainted, my brother and I clutched father's long legs. It was an unforgettable moment. People who were standing around us joined in crying and some of them muttered: "Ha, les sales Boches!"

"Les salauds!" We were given something to drink and father told how he and mother had given up all hope of finding us alive. They had been roaming about for days.

They had asked ambulances to stop, and when the door had been opened for them, they had recoiled in horror, because in there had been lying many wounded, dying children. The bombardments had been succeeding each other quickly and for them it had been certain that we had been irretrievably lost.

My Five Little Clouds In The Sky

In my class there were five Jewish girls. I was the only one to survive the war. Why me? In order to preserve their memories?

Shall I tell you about little Rose Hollander, or Maria Millstein, Esther Lovensmith or Henriette Neuman?

Their small faces are engraved on my mind, as are their names. Shall I first tell you about Henriette? Henriette fascinated me. She lived just around the corner and her parents kept an old dingy little hat shop . Henriette looked like a fat, ruddy Angora cat. She had light brown eyes with golden sparkles and her mouth, which was soft and pink, was always laughing. God was her great obsession. When we walked home from school together, she unremittingly talked about God, hell and damnation. Also, she could talk solemnly about God. Sometimes she said, "God is everywhere, He sees everything and everybody." And for the first time I heard about hell and purgatory and bodies that everlastingly burn there…Henriette was a child with a powerful imagination. So she would sometimes say, brooding, "God is everywhere; He always stands next to us, even in the toilet…" Afterward, I didn't dare to take off my pants for a long time, because I felt ashamed of God standing next to me in the toilet, watching how I relieved myself, as all people do. I was standing there for a long time with stomach-ache and a high tide but did not dare to let down my pants, as He was standing there, He was everywhere, even in the toilet…

Then, one day, I saw how the Neuman family was taken away by the Germans. Henriette was sitting in the truck. She waved to me and gave me one of her cheerful smiles. She was setting out on a journey, a big adventure, and the whole family was going with her. Why should she be scared? The sun was shining on her ruddy hair and spinning golden threads through it; in her arms she held a brown teddy-bear and her mouth was sucking at something sweet. Again she closely resembled a ruddy cat, blinking its eyes in the sunlight.

I waved, bye Henriette, bye Henriette, bye…Hen…riet…te…

Long after the ghost-truck had vanished from sight, I was still standing there. I felt profoundly sad, because I felt that Henriette had gone away forever. She would never again tell me those exciting stories…But…God was standing near her; she did not need to be scared!…

Whenever I think of Maria Millstein, the sad feeling of desertion overpowers me. The feeling of being deceived by life, for a friend so sincere as Maria I have never known again…

In my memories I see her as a fat well-fed girl, and at the same time I see her walking with me on a sunny summer day before the war. The streets were broiling hot, the two of us were on our way to the town park. She spoke wisely, Maria, with the words of her mother! While talking she bit into a pear. The juice ran down from the corners of her mouth, seeped into her little décolleté and left behind a shining line on her light-brown skin. I still hear the scream of dismay, I still see the look of disgust on her face, for in her hand Maria held half a pear with in the middle of it a twisting yellow worm, which she had bitten in two.

My first encounter with Maria was sheer coincidence. I had accompanied father, who then also met her parents for the first time. While I was sitting on the edge of my chair, I looked about the room and thought they were rich people. They had a bowl with goldfish and Maria had her own room!

While the mother offered me a piece of cake, she said: "Go and play with Maria…" We looked at each other and our little inner radars came into operation. Should I? Would she? Maria smiled a bit seriously and she nodded slightly in the direction of her room. Her eyes said "come". Speechless I watched her collection of dolls, and Maria told me that after the summer holidays she would go to school in the Quellin street. "That's my school," I exclaimed, "so then we're going together!" The ice was broken and we were friends. She often came to me, and once she told me how she had got a little brother who had died on the way, when they emigrated from Poland. Her voice sounded hoarse with emotion, when she spoke about the birth of her little brother. The room had been full of blood-stains, a doctor and a nurse had walked about with blood on their hands, she had heard her mother yell terribly, and her screams she had heard all over the neighborhood. That was the first time I heard that giving birth to children was painful. And we swore to each other that we should never have children.

Dear, serious Maria, she was an only child, her parents' idol, an excellent pupil at school. She obtained excellent marks and had a beautiful hand-writing that I was madly jealous of.

When the darkest period of our life came and we were reduced to human game, both our fathers were called up, and together they left for a labor camp. Maria stayed alone with her mother and we met less and less often. Many Jewish families had already been taken away, when, one day, Maria came and rang the door bell. Her mother had been away for many hours. It was nearly seven o'clock, and after that hour Jews were no longer allowed on the streets. Maria was very upset, she cried and was seized by panic that an accident might have happened to her mother. Had she been caught in a razzia? The next morning Maria wandered about looking for her mother, who had still not yet returned. Again she called at our door and mother advised her to go to the Jewish committee, which was then located in the

Lange Leem street. Maybe they could tell her what had become of her mother.

On the way there she was picked up during a razzia. She was taken to Mechelen, from where she was transported further to Auschwitz. After the war, when mother had returned from the camps, she told me that in Auschwitz Maria had been assigned to that group of children who, immediately upon arrival, had been sent to heaven via the chimney of the crematorium.

I have to tell you about little Esther! She too was living in our street, next to the green-grocer's, exactly half-way between Maria and me. I did not like little Esther that much, but she was extremely fond of me. In the morning she always rang our door bell and then I begged mother to go to the window and give her a sign to indicate that I had already left. Mother did so every time. She opened the window and signified with a wave of her hand that I had already left. I preferred the company of Maria or Henriette... Esther was an untidy child, from a very untidy family. Her mother had been married a couple of times, and in between she had used up a few lovers. Out of those many affairs came many children and you simply lost count when you tried to find out just how many little brothers and sisters Esther really had.

When you passed by the ground floor where the family was living, you could often hear them quarrel from the street; sometimes the mother pushed a few children out of the house and threw a bucket of water over them to cool them down. She was a fascinating woman with golden teeth and unkempt hair.

But little Esther was a slight child. She had a submissive expression in her big lack lustre eyes. As a matter of fact, everything about her was big. Her mouth with the protruding teeth, her hands and feet, but her intelligence was small, and so was mine. So the two of us were always at the tail of the prize-giving.

Actually, she was a little sweetheart, little Esther, but she was always smelling of garlic and sometimes I felt a bit guilty when mother had sent her away and she ran out of the street in the hope of catching up with me after all and go to school together. I was usually waiting nicely for my other friend. She never saw through it, fortunately; she kept calling and running, faithfully, every day.

But...she couldn't run any more when the truck of the Gestapo was in front of her door...She couldn't run as she was pushed barefoot into the shower which released gas instead of water. Not one of the 6 million who were doomed to death, was able to run. Little Esther did not have to run, for the pits had already been dug. And she, little Esther—I can imagine—hardly took any room; she was so narrow, so slight.

Only my pain has remained.

Can we, may we forget them?

On purpose I kept little Rose Hollander to the last; for little Rose was not really my friend. She was far too intelligent! She was always the first in the class, and at every question of Miss she raised her hand. She used to sit at the desk in front of me and while I was looking at her back, I dreamed away in many wonderful adventures.

Little Rose looked like a flushing red apple. She had deep set brown eyes and two thick long tresses hung on her back. She used to wear those beautiful gay dresses, and my gaze ever wandered through the window toward the magnificent lime tree and the fragment of blue sky which was hardly visible. When I looked in front of me again, I was staring once more on little Rose's back, gaily decorated with big pink naps, which made your mouth water, because they reminded you of the pink sweets for 25 centimes in the little shop around the corner. The little ships carried me away to foreign countries over the sea and the flowers lured my thoughts to a distant paradise where everything existed, except the class and the boring life. The stern voice of Miss brought me back to reality. And dear God, poor thing, if you were suddenly called to the blackboard after such a lovely dream…What a disaster. Most often I would stand there with a dazed look. The green blackboard with the wriggling white letters moving like snakes, and in my hand the little stub of chalk, which I dropped through sheer nervousness and which accidentally rolled away as far as the feet of the angry Miss, who finally screamed out the liberating word: "Sonia Blumenstein, get out…" At last, I, Sonia, happily leaving the classroom, free at last to go on dreaming in peace…Was not the corridor a dungeon, the school a centuries old castle? Everything was cold and wet, green and mildewed. The coats on the pegs, were they not hanged beheaded corpses?…I lived in a pink world on another planet…

My dreams mingled with the delicious smell of the vegetable soup, that came from the school-porter's kitchen. Almost 12 o'clock, almost the liberating bell that would bring you outside, where Maurice would be waiting, my little friend who lived opposite.

Maurice would carry my book bag and little Rose would walk behind us, green with envy. For little Rose was in love with Maurice, and Maurice with me, and I?...

I was in love with father, of course!

When by the end of 1942 a razzia was held in our neighborhood, they drove me into the synagogue too. The street was suddenly empty and deserted. Shots rang out. People were not allowed to come to the window. They fired when a curtain moved. The Gestapo fired at the slightest movement. The synagogue was full of people. Old men stood praying. Women and children anxiously looked about. Babies were crying, black and green uniforms. Strong men were guarding defenseless people, and there all at once, I saw little Rose Hollander. She looked pale, her eyes terrified, I felt a sweaty hand. "Sonia, have you been run in as well?" she asked. The urgent sound of her voice made me suddenly realize that my life was in danger. All at once the same fear fell upon me as it had upon her, and in panic I heard her voice as if from afar, like a soft whisper. "My pussy cat, what will become of my pussy cat?" I laid my hand on her shoulder and said soothingly: "I will look after your pussy cat." She looked at me gratefully and gave me a kiss on my cheek. I pushed through the rows of people until I was close to the gate, and slipped outside, carefree past the men of the Gestapo and sneaking past the houses.

As I rang the door bell, mother quickly pulled me inside. Angrily, she slapped me a couple of times. How dared I run into the streets during the razzia? I did not dare to tell her where I had been, and what I had seen. Later, when I was lying in my bed, I thought of little Rose. What was going to happen to her pussy cat? I had completely forgotten to ask her address. The next day I walked by the synagogue, no one there, nothing but silence. Nothing was left of the hundreds of people who had been brought together there and carried off in trucks afterward.

And little Rose? Only a name, a wisp of a little cloud in the blue sky...Over there, look, in the far distance you see Henriette and Maria and little Esther and you see that new school which has no memories linked to it.

The Star

Frocks with flowers, fishes, forests, heath. The girls who were sitting in front of me have never been able to imagine what wonderful adventures happened on their backs. Sometimes Miss called: "Come, Sonia, you write the result of that problem on the blackboard." Then I was standing there with failing knees, and while I was looking at that monstrous blackboard, its green color spread out to make room for all sorts of crazy shapes that made me laugh. And because Miss saw this, I was thrown out, to my great relief. Then I got a new friend, as stupid as I was, her name was Flor. We were just having needlework when Florentin Verbraeken came into the classroom. She was tremendously tall and as lean as a rake. She had a plain freckled face and on her left cheek a big brown birthmark, as if a big mouse was stuck on her cheek. That is why she got the nickname "the mouse". Florentin became a mystery to me, I saw her come and go, and she talked and played with nobody. I began to study her and one day she received a severe scolding from Miss. When we came out into the playground at 10 o'clock she sat down on a bench and started to cry. It was no ordinary crying, sobbing and sniveling. No, she was sitting with an impenetrable face while tears were running out of her eyes just like that, without making any noise. A great pity for her surged up in me. I sat down by her and put my hand on her hand and while very upset about myself, we stayed there silently until the bell rang and she gave me her arm, after which we went upstairs. In the classroom I kept peeping at her and when our looks crossed each other, she smiled quietly, almost happily.. All of a sudden that mouse had disappeared from her face and I saw her beautiful grey eyes and her well-shaped mouth. I was overwhelmed.

Florentin had changed entirely since I had seen her laughing. At 4 o'clock we went home. It became our habit to go out of our way along the Keizerlei, so that we could be longer together. On Wednesday afternoon she came to play with me. I felt ashamed because of the untidy house, but, in fact, it was a dream-house for children. No one ever shouted: "wipe your feet," or "be careful not to dirty anything." No, the children were masters of everything. We played at hide-and-seek in the wardrobe and cops-and-robbers on the beds. Cleaning did not exist for mother, and the biggest quarrels arose because mother was so careless. She took it for granted that father should bring her coffee in bed and wash and dress us, and get us off to school.

She could stay in bed for hours with a three-penny novel and if, by any chance, a visitor came at noon, mother had not had the time to cook dinner. Florentin was the laughter of my childhood, she taught me how to laugh at the most stupid things: boys who whistled at us, a dog that relieved itself, a man we saw stumbling, the teachers became the craziest caricatures through her. And again it was little Flor who helped me get over the first great humiliation.

Once I came home from school and saw a big yellow piece of cloth with stars on the table. "Father," I asked, "what's that for?" "Sonny," father said, "tomorrow you're going to school with a star on your dress and on your coat. You're no longer allowed to come on the streets without that star, that's punishable!

"Me? Me, with a star on my clothes to school? Why father? The children will laugh at me and…" "Sonny," father said, "listen carefully. It is absolutely no shame to wear that star, we are Jews and we should be proud to wear that star." But I could not be proud and in my mind I saw myself entering the school, gazed at by all my classmates and Florentin would no longer be my friend and would feel ashamed to walk in the streets with me. I felt deeply unhappy and would not listen to comforting words. I felt ashamed to go to school with that yellow piece of cloth.

In the morning, I saw dozens of stars in the streets and suddenly I saw how many Jews were living in our neighborhood. At school I had never noticed the difference between Jewish and non-Jewish children. We sat at the same desks, learned the same lessons, we were practically the same children.

Only the names made you realize for one moment; that one is a Jew!

Never shall I forget the humiliation I felt as I entered the school and suddenly saw two different races. The race with and the race without a star. Many children were watching me and I thought; they will see my heart beat under that damned star. I was not proud, I was unhappy when a girl asked me astonished: "Sonia, are you a Jew as well?" I could not answer and I hoped that I would drop dead.

All of a sudden Florentin came toward me, held out her hand to me and said: "Come on, Son." I pushed her hand away from me and said: "Leave me, Flor, leave me alone." There I was sitting and I felt the looks of the girls and it seemed to me as if I were not washed, as if I were dirty and soiled. With that star my life had changed abruptly. I did not look at anybody any more, I refused to look into Florentin's begging eyes during the lesson, I left the school with my head raised. All of a sudden, Florentin came after me. "Come on, Son, don't be so silly. We'll walk home together, as always." I said: "Please go away. Go to those others. We can't be friends any longer. I am wearing a star and if you walk with me, the others will pester you and I don't want that." Then little Flor said, "Son, you've got to stay my friend and I'm proud that you are my friend." Then I gave her a kiss and she gave me her arm and together we ran home. All at once I had forgotten about my star and my being Jewish. Little Flor was there and she was proud to be my friend. The whole world could explode, little Flor remained my friend.

But after some time, we Jewish children were shut out by the others. They did not let us play together and we stood apart in little groups. Little Flor too was expelled by the non-Jewish children and when I asked her once: "Aren't you sorry that you took my side?", then she answered smilingly, "A fat lot I care." And her smile changed into a deep laugh, so that the birthmark on her cheek nearly touched her eye.

After the war I met her mother. She had grown old and grey.

Little Flor had been hit by a V-bomb. She was just 14.

The Kaufman Family

Again I heard the song "Silent Night, Holy Night". It is early this year, I thought. It is getting earlier every year. In our streets there stands a Christmas tree at every house, and by the Christmas tree you can tell what kind of people live in that house. Next to us they have a tree in the shape of a snake. One thin arrow with a few projections, which are decorated with one single scanty little lamp. Opposite there is a tree which nearly sags with all the ornaments. On top shines a silver star. It is peculiar that the people next to us are extremely slender and the neighbors opposite nicely fat. It is the star opposite which every year gives me that miserable feeling during the Christmas period.

In 1942 I was also looking opposite. For hours I could watch as if fascinated how the neighbours were sitting sociably around the Christmas tree. With my nose against the cold window, I was watching the silver star, the daughter was playing the piano. It was just like a scene from a film.

The night before Christmas, Helene Kaufman as well as her parents and her little brother were taken out of the house. They were living right next to that Christmas tree. Peace on earth to all men of good will. Helene Kaufman was a 12-year-old fat girl. She was the exact image of her mother; short nape, short legs and they both had an abnormally long upper body. The mother moved as the daughter did and the daughter as her mother. Slow were their actions. They always had time. It was as if they were practicing rhythmic dancing. On Sabbath they set the table in the dining room. The tablecloth was white and the silver candlestick was glittering in the middle of the table. But the way in which they put down the plates and dishes was like a play. There was something exaggerated about it. The curtains were always open and it looked as if they were performing a comedy for the neighbors. I always resented the sight of the father and his little son praying. They shook so heavily that their noses nearly touched the plates. The father then broke a piece of challe and he divided it, after which they put the little piece into the salt and said the beroche. They always behaved so stiffly, in such a dignified and superior way. Sometimes they also looked through the window, but she would never have nodded. Maybe her neck was too short?

It was the sudden noise, the breaking of glass and the shouting of Germans "Fort machen, schnell!", that woke me up and made me run toward the window. I saw how the Germans were pushing the Kaufman family—with only a coat over their night clothes—into the Black Maria. They were beating them, because even now, they were slow. Each of them was carrying a small case. The mother and Helene were crying, the father was praying...After silence had returned to the street, I saw the star glittering. The colored lamps produced a cheerful sight and it was snowing. The snow covered the footprints of father, mother, Helene and little Kaufman and the footprints of the Germans as well.

Babbe

"Sonia," Mamma said, "never answer the front door, last night there was a razzia in the Van Lerus street." It was 1943...

One week later, I was playing my favorite game in the hall. The blanket I was sitting on became a big ballroom, my dolls became princes and princesses. Crystal chandeliers were shining at the ceiling. I was in my dreamworld where there was no war, no Gestapo, no hunger, no fear and no persecution...I had, for one moment, become a normal child again and so I spontaneously opened the front door when the bell rang.

There in front of me stood the Gestapo. With a shock I realized that Babbe could not escape any more and that we could not hide her in the large wardrobe as we used to do when we heard there was going to be a razzia. Being a Russian, she had a Russian passport. But, good Lord, it was too late. Then came mother and she showed her Belgian passport...

But over there in the corridor they saw Babbe move behind the glass door and she was taken out of the kitchen. Never shall I forget her crying, her screaming and begging when she was dragged through the corridor to the Black Maria. She was like a little heap of misery. All my life I shall be haunted by her brown eyes that looked at me strangely...For it was I who had opened the door...

Mother clung to the car, she cried terribly. "Sign," the Gestapo man said, "then you can, as well as your children, accompany your mother, then you can stay together after all." I saw mother grasping for the pen. All at once my Babbe stood up; she looked like a proud statue with shining eyes and with pointing hand she ordered mother not to sign. "Think of the children," she shouted.

I stood looking at my Babbe, fascinated, my eyes clung to her. I knew, another few minutes and I should never see her again. I felt it all over and there was so much more I had to tell her: How I loved her, how lonely I would be without her, that I was the sugar thief who always stole her lumps and that it was I who had been sneaking from her little jam jars.

That I would suffer from the cold at night without her old body near me in the large bed. That she still had not completely taught me the evening prayer. Who would teach me the rest of it if Babbe were no longer here? And who would take care of our food and who would put warm glasses on my back when I got ill, as I was every winter...Who could comfort me as Babbe could? But not a noise passed my rigid lips.

I realized that I would live through those images a thousand times over and over again, as long as I live, as long as I live...

When the car began to move, I heard her cry, "Fourteen children I have born and now I have to go to death alone..." I still see her before me and I see her in every old woman I meet. She was standing there with her pointed shawl on her thin hair, wide-eyed with dismay, her fists clenched, praying to God whom she, however devout she was, did not understand at that moment, because she was kind to a fault. She always lived for others...I heard her curse Hitler, a name she always pronounced with "pooh", while she spat, usually without spittle. When her cursing turned into wailing, the car began to move. Her body shook, she fell, I saw how she raised herself against the railing to look at me once more...

Her last look has pursued me for years, I shall never forget her eyes...That is the way she was torn away from us, my poor good Babbe, on her journey to Auschwitz.

After she had gone, I cried out my sorrow in her handkerchiefs. In her pillows I sought for her smell like an animal. I caressed her old familiar belongings, cherished them, as if I already knew then that I, too, had to leave everything behind, because nothing of Babbe has remained. Only I remember how she was, that little old Russian Babbe with her "kartoffel latkes" and red "Börst", with her Yiddish-Russian accent, with her songs of "Beigelech" and "Meidelech" and "oif dem prippitiek brent a faierell", and "Bérele" and her fingers crooked from doing the laundry…and her little smiles that could warm you up inside as if you suddenly saw the sun shining in winter and you knew for certain that after all it would become spring again.

In my life remorse will always grow with me, because I opened the door and let the Gestapo come in…

Beardie

After a few months at Saint-Omer we grew homesick and went back to Antwerp. As we had left it, we found our house back.

> "Two days after my death nobody will talk about me; that is
> why you have to be of some weight while you are still here."
> *Herman Van Veen*

My personal feelings are summarized in these few words. I feel within me that fear of dying suddenly. I have made myself a promise. I want to revive my family; those who died in the crematorium, who turned from man into smoke. A few of those 6 million I want to revive…After all these years I still cannot understand why all this has happened. That slaughter of millions of innocent people.

Thus, I recently smelled the odor of fried white herring. War and white herring go together and I suddenly thought of that evening, how we were turned out on the streets. The people with whom we had stayed underground had become afraid and we wandered about and there was nowhere we could go to. I remember how apathetic mother was when she decided to go back to our house, in the Terlist street. Actually, that was a spontaneous surrender to the Gestapo, because there were no more Jews in our Jewish quarter.

You could tell by the houses, you felt by the paving stones. The neighborhood was deserted, without life, as if everything was mourning, as if fear and pain were hiding in every corner.

Like three thieves we slipped into the house, mother, my little brother and I. The house where we had once been so happy, each room with its memories, the house was empty, the Arthur Pierre removers had plundered it completely.

But, being children and glad to be home again, we forgot the war for a while and we ran from one room into the other as if we expected to find something back from former days. We found a small, rusty gas cooker. We carried it upstairs to our former kitchen and mother fried white herring. We slept on the bare floor where once the dining room used to be. We lay close to mother, who was crying softly all night long...

On the corner there was a grocery shop, mother was there when the Gestapo truck stopped in front of our house. It was nearly noon. They hammered on the front door. They shouted: "Mach auf, Jude!" With my heart in my mouth, I opened the door. The Gestapo stood in front of me, that one too, the most fearsome. He used to be called: "Beardie". He commanded: "Passport!" I told him mother had just left and that we expected her back soon. All six of them searched the house. We had to show them to the loft. They searched the roof, they thought to find more Jews there. At last, they left, urging us not to leave the house, for they would take us away when mother came home.

Next to us there was a bawdy house. While they were paying a visit there mother crossed the street, seized us and we ran...ran for our lives. We jumped on tram 12 and reached the house of a family which later, when our money ran out, delivered us up to the Gestapo. Later we heard that a reward had been offered to the one who found us. "Beardie" had raised the devil when they discovered we had escaped.

"Beardie" was known as a real sadist. He beat people, pulled out old Jews' beards. A story went the rounds, which must have happened in the Kievit street, with a certain Jacobovitz family, whose newborn baby he had thrown out of the first floor window into the truck.

It was a gloomy day in 1942 when, as a 12-year-old girl, I stood under the Leopold Bridge watching how the holy scriptures were taken out of the synagogue and set on fire in enormous piles. I stood there and saw the old men reaching into the fire with trembling hands in order to save some Talmud books. I saw the fire leaping high and slipping along the parchment scrolls like hungry tongues, then everything turned to ashes.

Through my tears I saw the old men crying. Their heads bent and with drooping shoulders. I felt such pity for them, my people, my blood—there was nothing I could do. I stood paralyzed, watching this smarting scene. Then they were carried away in the trucks by the Germans. And as in a fairy tale...The years went by and a new synagogue was built. Once more you can see old "Babbes" praying during the Sabbath; once more you see little children playing on the stairs, in the corridor and in the street...Meanwhile their parents pray God to ask for health, happiness, merit and peace. They pray to a God whom they fear and love at the same time; a God who punishes them and selected them as a chosen people to suffer...

The Cane Portmanteau

Sometimes I am confronted with young people who cannot understand that we let ourselves be led up to the slaughter like lambs. I try to tell them about the refined plan the Germans carried out. How they first called up the young men, under the pretext they were sent to a labor camp.

My father too, received a summons for the "Organization Tott". In town word got round that, if men did not answer the summons and so refused, punitive measures would be taken against their families.

Father shrugged his shoulders and said: "I am still young. I can work..." In the morning we went to S...and bought a cane portmanteau. I had seen many men leave with such a cane portmanteau, and now also my father. We were not allowed to be with them when he said good-bye to mother. I heard her sobbing in the bedroom.

My little brother and I were standing on the pavement. My brother was still small, hardly 7 years old, he understood that father had to leave but he did not cry. He looked at his shoes and when father said that he should be a good boy in times to come, he nodded "Yes". Now that father went away he was the man in the house, wasn't he? He laughed about the joke father made, gave him a kiss and ran away to play. But for me it was a solemn moment. I had to promise always to look after my little brother. I had to pledge my word. While I nearly choked with tears and with great difficulty made my sacred promise, I looked into the face that was so dear to me. How green his eyes were...How long would he stay away? Maybe I would not recognize him later. I looked for a distinctive mark in his face, something real, something tangible. I was desperate when he turned round and said that I could not come to the station with him. I had to stay behind, upset, broken. But when he had turned the corner, I followed him. I saw him walking. Erect band proud. I hated that cane portmanteau. It did not fit in with father. I followed him as far as the station and there I lost him in the crowd.

Later I looked for him in every man I met, one single distinctive mark...eyes, mouth. Always looking for something by which I could recognize him, the tall, beautiful Prince Charming.

Nobody knows what exactly happened to him. One says that he was assigned to a group which had to fetch archives from burning houses for the Germans in Poland. Others say that he died during a bombardment in Poland. According to my mother, he belonged to a group of 100 men who had to dig their own graves, after which they were shot.

Anyhow, father was pushed into the train in Mechelen and that train sped off...

Father said... "When you are grown up, we'll go to the ball together and I'll dance the first dance with you. You'll wear a white satin dress with lace hems and little pink flowers. When you are grown up, you'll have a prince..."

"Look, I have planted violets in the garden. Violets have little faces..."

How tall father was in my eyes and how small I was in his.

Spring '43

Spring 1943. In the air a silent promise, a sweet joy spread among the people, will there be peace at last? In the warbling of birds, in their songs you heard the coming of beautiful days. You looked at the trees and you saw the little green leaves that after all sprouted again like every year after a cold winter. You hoped, you dreamed, you prayed that your most ardent wish could be granted. Peace, dear God, give us PEACE at last. For one year already we had been underground with a family in Deurne and we were running out of money. Mother was becoming desperate..

We could not pay the 13000 francs plus the extra food coupons any longer. By coincidence we got an address in the Leopold street, from a man who supported Jews in hiding. Actually, we did this on the off-chance, because sometimes Jews were caught that way! It could be a trap. But we had no other choice, we had to find a way to get some money. That day we decided to ask for help. We came out of our hiding place. The house was in the Van Rijen street (n° 48), we went down the Confortalei and waited for the tram at the greengrocer's shop, opposite the pharmacy "Drie Torekes". Suddenly two men appeared dressed in dark overcoats and felt hats. They looked at us and nodded. A great fear fell over me; I had noticed that look of mutual understanding. When finally tram 12 arrived, they got in too and stayed close by us. In a low voice I said to mother: "Ma, we have been betrayed!" Mother went pale as death—she had understood. At the Leopold street we got off and one of the men commanded: "Passport!" Mother passed her Belgian passport with the red "Jude" stamp. They pushed us into the passage of a vacant house, controlled our papers, constantly threatening us with a revolver. They took us along to the "Harmonie" where at that time the "Sicherheitsdienst" was put up. They showed us politely into a waiting room and we sat there anxiously, guarded by two feldgendarmen. In the adjoining room a lot of activity was going on, the telephone kept ringing, loud voices were shouting orders.

All at once we were called inside and there, for the first time, I saw those eyes. The figure in the wheelchair spoke fluently Dutch and German. I cannot remember whether he wore a green or a black uniform. Was he Belgian or German? I only remember how he was sitting there. A crumpled figure with a hump, piercing grey eyes and a big voluptuous mouth. Sneering, he ordered us to sit down. During the formalities he observed me attentively. I was 13, well built and in my knitted dress I looked 16. "Sign," he said to mother. "Sign, that your daughter is 16, then she can come along to Mechelen." "No," mother said, "she is just a child, she is only 13, and I won't sign." The hunchback grinned and suddenly he said to mother in German: "That little pigeon is for me tonight." Mother jumped to her feet and shouted: "Kill us, kill us rather than inflict this upon us!"" At that moment mother seemed a real heroine to me! We were taken away while the hunchback laughed at me, sneeringly.

We were locked up in a small corner room where only two persons could stand upright. In front of the door we heard the boots of a guard who was walking up and down. Very clearly I still remember that I was crying hysterically. I begged mother to sign and to take me along to Mechelen. She could not leave me behind all by myself...What would happen to me? I felt a fear beyond description, I desperately clung to her, kissed her, begged her not to leave me alone. But mother kept exceptionally calm. She caressed my hair and she had a strange voice when she said: "It's all over now anyhow! For so long we have kept up and right now, now that the war is nearly over, now they have caught us and now we shall surely die, don't be afraid, for afterward we shall meet again, everyone we have loved; our whole family." She could not comfort me with her words. "Mama," I cried, "I'm only 13, I don't want to die! I want to live, live! Let me go with you, let me..." That night in that little den we endured an awful amount of fear. Every time the boots of the guard stopped at our door, we thought they had come to get us; for had he not said: "that little pigeon is for me tonight…"?

In the morning they took us away. It may have been 4 o'clock. There was a truck at the front door and we were loaded into it. They took me to the Jewish orphanage in the Lange Leem street and mother to the prison in the Begijnen street.

Shall I ever be able to forget that drive? That beautiful pale sky, that awakening morning with here and there a dwindling star. Silent, sleeping streets; my Antwerp. How dear to me all this was. How intensely I lived at that moment. We threw our jewels in the street, tender memories of father, a birthday present, a beautiful watch, gold earrings with rubies, a ring. Mother said: "It is better that someone picks this up than that the Germans take it away from us." How distressed I was when I threw away those presents from father. When the truck stopped in front of the orphanage, I embraced mother for a long time and I sobbed out: "Mama, when shall we ever meet again? And where?" She answered: "In heaven, perhaps…" She did not cry as I did and there seemed to be no fear like my fear for the future yet to come. I was delivered at the orphanage.

David

I remember how compassionately I had once looked at the poor orphan children. That was a few months before. I had looked into the spacious dining room and there I had seen children of different ages. I had found it a sad sight the way they had been playing with each other. So many children without parents, I had thought at that time. And now I was standing there myself, an orphan, in front of the green front door of the orphanage and I could hardly believe that now I was one of them. I was taken into the office and the headmistress, Madame Rothschild, looked at me anxiously. "Did they hurt you?" she gently asked. "Did they beat you, were you ill-treated?" "No," I said and I did not understand why she watched me so attentively. At that moment I did not realize what I looked like. Now I remember…My eyes were swollen from crying and from standing in the little den with mother all night. And the tears kept rolling out of my eyes while she was speaking with me, they could not be stopped, fresh tears were added all the time…I felt so sorry for myself, an orphan among orphans. Then the headmistress took me to the children who were staring at me large eyed—a new one! I sat down on a bench in the corner and watched my new surroundings. Everything seemed so sad to me, the wooden tables, the long narrow wooden benches, the chagrined-looking children around me.

They played without making any noise, that is what I found so strange. It was as if they were afraid of the outside world, as if they were afraid to be heard or to be noticed through the walls, if they dared make any noise. The Lange Leem street was a gloomy street at that time, like most of the streets in the Jewish quarter, where the houses had been looted and destroyed. It looked as if the town were grieving at the deportation of thousands of Jews. Sometimes the sun shone over the vacant houses, but there was no warmth, no life behind the bare, cheerless windows that looked into the streets like big eyes. The street, where people walked close by the houses, afraid of the Germans and afraid of the approaching bombardments... Only in the centre, near the station, you saw some signs of life. The cinemas showed films of Sarah Leander and Marika Röckk.

But in the orphanage we were not allowed to go through the large glass door which separated us from the corridor and the street. Nobody dared to ignore this severe order. Besides, where should we have gone to? I remember the first day and David. David was praying in a corner with his prayer coat on. He, too, had been brought to the orphanage the day before, after the Gestapo had discovered his mother and his little sister in a vacant house in the Plantijn-en-Moretuslei. For months they had been able to hide themselves in the back part of the house, an old servant had regularly brought them food. Surprised, I looked at David who, wrapped up in his prayer, seemed to forget the world. Time and again he bent forward against the wall, cried in a hoarse voice and begged God for help. The songs were monotonous and his black curls hung over his high forehead and covered his dark brown eyes. His narrow lips were moving as if in a fever, nobody besides myself looked at him, and I wondered how you could pray so piously, so passionately, how you could believe in God so intensely, while He had left us, had deceived us, while He let us all die. And I? I too would die!!!...I felt it. While David was praying, I swore. God be damned!

When the evening fell, I was allotted a bed. I received a coarse cotton nightshirt and because I was very shy, I undressed in the toilet. I was surprised that the other children let their clothes slip down and that they were standing stark naked in front of each other, quite shameless. I felt miserable and I could have died of shame, just by looking at them. When I was lying in bed, I realized that nobody had spoken to me. I was a miserable lump of loneliness and in the twilight I started softly to sob. I do not know what fell upon me at that moment. Had I suddenly become mad? For I did something which I have never understood of myself later on. The bedroom was quiet, here and there a child was whispering, and all at once I began to call for my father. Silently at first, then louder and louder and at the same time I was sobbing my heart out. They sent for the headmistress and she came to sit near me, she caressed me, washed my face with cold water and spoke in a soft hushing tone. She said I should be calm and that father had gone, like all the fathers of the many children. But I was inconsolable, I cried for father almost hysterically. "Papa," I cried, "come and get me, please don't leave me alone here, I want to get away from here." The headmistress' old father also came to sit near me and I clung to him, convinced that father had come. He took me with him, I do not know what had got into me at that time. They took me up and I was brought into a little room somewhere in the house. While I was going upstairs, I cried: "Papa, I'm coming, I'm coming." I was in a state of shock for days. The doctor who came by could not tell a thing. Emotions…he said.

While I was lying there in the little room for days, alone, isolated from the other children, I heard David praying. I heard the humming life in me. I heard whispering voices anxiously talking about me. The days went by and I did not have the least desire to leave my loneliness. I was happy in that seclusion. I was so frightened of the many unknown children who stared at me and did not speak to me.

Then one day we heard that the orphanage had to move. A feverish excitement took possession of everybody; and I was totally forgotten. That is why I went downstairs, driven by hunger, found myself in the dining room and sat down at the table to eat with the others, in my nightshirt. From then on I got better and David became my friend. David, who asked for my attention with all sorts of little assiduities. David, who carried my parcel during the journey to Lasne. David, who made sure that I sat comfortably. ate well and David, who fell in love with me in the loutish way of a 15-year-old.

The 16 children who had been brought in last, survived the war with an even greater fear than the others. We were always ready to be fetched by the Gestapo. That we stayed alive, those last 16, I ascribe to the many inexplicable miracles which were reserved for some during the war. We stayed alive thanks to the "White Brigade" which destroyed the papers of the 16 children.

In me something is growing which is beyond description. I believe it is an overwhelming feeling of gratitude towards life itself. That I am a chosen one and that I was allowed to stay alive after the most dreadful slaughter of all times.

Neither shall I ever get rid of that feeling of guilt I have toward my mother. When our country was liberated and when dancing, rejoicing people were marching through the capital, we, the "five girls", were at the orphanage in Auderghem. We suddenly realized that there would come a new phase in our lives. No more fear of the Gestapo, no more hunger, cold, misery. Life was full of adventure, we were in the middle of it and lived. In silence we cursed the headmistress, who did not allow us to experience that flush of joy. The Americans who were embraced and snowed under with flowers, the giddy crowd which marched through the streets singing. We had to stay in the orphanage. We heard the messages over the radio: so and so looking for family; prisoner of war looking for any possible family. We heard the messages, shrugged our shoulders and acted as if we were not interested. Who could still hope? We knew that those without rich relatives in America who could take up a child, would be sent to Israel, to another orphanage or kibbutz.

The mere thought of it at that time made me shudder. In my mind I made up a plan to escape with my brother. For us it would never be Israel.

Sonia, Someone Is Looking For You

We heard names and names until suddenly a girl claimed to have heard the name Blumenstein. She came to me and called out happily: "Sonia, someone is looking for you." My first thought was, father, or aunt, or uncle, but that it could be mother did not enter my mind. I was very calm. The girls around me talked in low voices; in their hearts they were envying me. Until the last moment I did not know who it was, and then the day came when all of a sudden mother was standing before me. Was that mother? This skeleton? That carcass of 40 kilos, the hair shaved off and those long trousers and that jacket and those strange eyes? The least I should have done at that moment was faint. That was expected of me, I felt that. At least, I should have cried, and thrown myself into her arms. I knew all that, I knew what they were waiting for and what was expected of me, and I just stood there and did nothing.

Even now I could still set up a roar about it. How could I be so heartless? Finding mother back after Auschwitz and not reacting! Beside me there was a girl, Rachel. Her mother came out of the camp together with my mother. That girl was crying her eyes out and they held each other so tight as if they would never let go of one another and I who was just standing there...

All around us live silent heroes...heroes nobody talks about, who did not receive decorations and of whom you could never think that they were heroes. With pride I can say that my mother was such a quiet heroine, someone without fame or glory. Ma said abruptly: "Son, there is something I would like to tell you, about the past, when we were sent to Mechelen by the Gestapo. It happened at the time when I was still a human being, someone who still believed in humanity. There was one moment when I thought I would lose my mind..." Mother sighed deeply, and a deep line appeared between her violet-blue eyes..."Go on, tell me, ma" I encouraged her.

She began to tell...

"We, some 40 persons, would be transported to Mechelen. We knew that and yet we were so stupid as to believe that we would be able to put up some resistance. After all there were 40 of us!

"We arrived in Mechelen and there we were all subjected to a physical examination, in case we should hide arms...and then one by one we were sent into a little room. There were two SS-men, Belgians, one was Van Coppenolle, "the Horsehead" as he was called. Later he was sentenced to death. I had my shirt on and I had to take that off too. There I was standing stark naked.

"On the writing table was lying a big shining sword, I looked at it, fascinated, the horsehead made me stoop, legs spread wide open, more open, he ordered, and he looked, very deep into my genitals. Those cruel treatments were not only meant to humiliate us but mainly to find out whether we had not hidden any diamonds in there. Later I heard from other prisoners, that there were women who had done so. Then their rage was terrible. When that was discovered, the women were beaten up and tortured.

"Later, much later, when we were in Poland and before the cremations began, special women had to open the mouths of the dead to pull out their golden teeth and molars. Also the women's vaginas were examined to see whether anything was hidden there. All of those people had been gassed immediately upon their arrival in the camp.

"Inhuman scenes were enacted. The women who had to do that sinister job, sometimes discovered relatives or acquaintances among the corpses.

"While that was happening, child, I had to think of Babbe all the time, she must have experienced a similar fate and I did not feel the shame for myself, but I felt the shame because of my mother.

"After that we came into a hall where there were also other prisoners, who comforted us so that we might be able to forget. They spoke all sorts of comforting words, but I was so deeply humiliated, as a woman, as a human being, that I thought I would lose my mind. But people adjust themselves to the situation in which they end up.

"One day we were sent to Poland together with some 3,500 other Jews. In our coat we were carrying a knife, a file, something that was taken away with the idea of escape in mind. A German with a machine-gun was placed in our wagon.

"All the plans to jump the train fell to pieces. That train journey, in the cattle wagons, was beyond description for the stench and the dirt. We were forced to relieve ourselves on the train. Many old people died. We sat down on the dead, so as to be more comfortable and have a little more room. When we arrived in Poland, exhausted after all the misery we had gone through, large vans were standing ready to pick us up.

"Everybody pushed and wriggled to secure a seat, we were a group of 40 again, and we said: 'We're going to walk!' Was it instinct or was it coincidence? I heard someone say: "We have not come here to expect luxury," and that made me decide to walk with them.

"All those others were immediately taken from the vans to the gas chambers. We, the 40 of us, were taken to a room, where they totally shaved off our hair, in all places. When I was standing there with my bald skull, some executioners said: 'Sing! Those who can sing, get a good place.' A few urged me to sing and I sang more loudly and clearly than I had ever done before: 'Heut' ist der schönsten Tage in meinem Leben!'

"I had to clean the toilets. And it became a chain of hell and damnation. We got lice, our striped clothes were full of them. We became dulled: it did not hurt us any longer when, standing near the wash-houses, passing SS men forced us to wash ourselves naked. They watched us sniggering. During that awful winter too, they forced us to queue up naked in the snow. Those dogs were wearing fur coats and were beating their arms around their bodies because of the cold. We warmed ourselves by rubbing our bodies with snow. Many got pneumonia, many died.

"Again, we had to march for a long time, and as you know the Germans like discipline. There were prisoners who did not understand well their German commands, they did not march in time. Those became the victims of many blows with rifle butts that tore their skins open, clove their skulls and mostly they ended up in the gas chambers."

I looked at that little heap of humanity which was my mother and which had suffered because of her mother and an intense sorrow filled my heart. Maybe she has not deserved any decorations. From me she gets a large medal, because for me she is a heroine, as she was able to come back into society after such a hell and live as if it had only been a nightmare.

You, mother, are entitled to get all sorts of things which make you happy. I should have run towards you, held you tight and had a good cry on your drooping shoulders. But that is impossible. I can only look at you with eyes full of tears and a throat which does not let any spittle through. Poor, helpless mother, may my children make up for what I have failed to do. And to God I implore, let her stay with us for a long time yet, until all that remorse has died in me and teach me how to love her, so that she may still be a little happy in me.

At Night When I Wake Up

When I wake up at night and it seems to me that I hear somebody whisper: "Sonia, Sonia…" then I very quietly remain in bed and stream with perspiration and of course I know it is my imagination that plays me tricks, but that fear I feel is nothing compared to the fear they have felt in the gas chambers. It is that terror of the persecuted which has remained with me. While the air is grey and within me everything is so drab, I go through things which I don't like to write down, and yet I do so. Because afterward I shall savour the taste of deliverance, which is sweet and refreshing. There is not much that mother told about the camps. I used to ask: "Ma, how were things out there, what did you go through?" But mother never wanted to tell.

She used to say: "Ah…I have been through hell. I have already died once and it was worse than the very worst in the world," and after those words a great sadness welled up in me, because I shall forever and ever know myself imprisoned by the infinite compassion I felt for mother.

She has been in hell. And yet small fragments of conversations have lived on in me and sometimes it seems to me as if I had gone through it myself. Once mother went to a meeting of political prisoners. A memorial tablet was fixed on the door of the house where a girl, Maria Zimmetbaum, had lived.

She died as a heroine, mother told me. She tried everything to escape and when she had nearly succeeded, she was caught. In the camp the roll call was taken, all prisoners were brought together and Maria was hanged.

Her death was terrible because she spat in the SS men's faces. She was crying all the time: "Revenge, Revenge, Revenge." Until her throat was strangled.

Mother told me once about the big humiliations the women had to endure. In Poland the cold is terrible. There were nights that they had to stand on a square stark naked. For hours and hours in two long rows. In the morning the SS men came. Those whose skin showed eruptions were sent to the lethal chamber. The SS man's hand went right or left, those who went to the right came out through the chimneys of the crematorium.

From people they turned into smoke! Then mother told me that the worst was the crying of the young girls. They cried and begged, to be allowed to live one more day, one more hour. And what was even worse, there were mothers with daughters and it happened that the hand for the mother pointed to life, and the hand for the daughter to death. The mothers threw themselves in front of the hands and implored to take their lives instead of their children's. But the hand was inexorable.

We were going to have a new house again and I would be able to walk freely in the streets. I should not have to wear a star any longer and I was going to see Antwerp again. There was still a lot reserved for me in my life! Seeing my Antwerp again!!! Taking up life again after all those tribulations was not a simple task. The house was in a rotten condition. There was no light, no fire, no furniture, just the essentials of life that we got from the state. We ate bread and herring, and herring and bread. I do not believe that we were unhappy because of those things. The joy at being able to go about freely made up for a lot.

One night mother told me how she had escaped. "We were in Poland", she said, "we were brought together, about a thousand women. We only wore a long striped shirt to cover our nakedness, and those who walked in shoes or clogs were the privileged. They slept with the footwear in their arms, as if they were holding a baby, if not it would have been stolen from their feet. We went on foot from Poland to Germany, that journey had been called the dead-march, because very few have survived it. Food was not given any more at all. Along the way carrots and turnips were pulled out of the fields. This had to be done carefully, for if it was seen by the Kapo's, one was shot. At that time people died like flies. Those who sat down along the road were shot."

End

"There were four women who were always together. A German, Saidie, Sonia and I. Little by little we came into Germany where the scenery became hilly. We saw that we were near the end and we agreed to escape. One day we saw our way clear. The Kapo's stood talking together in panic. There was a landing in Normandy and they felt that the end of the war was near.

"The four of us suddenly let ourselves roll down a hill and ran on in desperation. They fired at us and we dropped down and remained motionless. The column went on. They thought we were dead.

"We arrived at an old farmhouse. It was deserted but we found some food. The evening fell and suddenly we heard drunken soldiers who spoke Russian. They knocked at the farmhouse and the German girl who was normally very ugly, was now really horrible. She said to us: 'Run away, I'll answer the door. They won't do anything to me, I'm too ugly,' and we jumped through a window and hid under a tree all night. In the beginning we heard her screams but later on nothing more. In the morning they left and we went in to see her. She was lying there on the floor, dead, raped." Sometimes, when I asked mother: "Tell me some more about what happened to you in the camp," then she would look at me with her lack lustre eyes. "You know," she said, "I suddenly think of that night they massacred the gypsies in the camp...

"We usually arrived in the camp at 7 o'clock. All day we worked in a munition plant. The Germans chased us into the barracks and they shouted: 'Blocksperre! Blocksperre!' That meant that we had to lie down on our plank beds and were not even allowed to go to the toilet. Or else we ran the risk of being shot. The evening fell, it was slowly getting dark. Suddenly we heard horrible cries from the gypsy camp. "I have to tell you about that camp," mother said, "An awfully dirty people was living there. They never had to work, we did not understand why. How could we know that they were doomed to death...

"We were used to seeing them messing about with their many children. For lack of hygiene they got into a filthy state. Thousands of gypsies were living in the camp and they were killed in an atrocious way. In one night they were all murdered."

I am trembling and although it is very warm in the room, I am cold. There reigns an uncomfortable silence and around mother, an air of terror; she sighs and her eyes darkly look into an even darker world that once belonged to her past...

"Thousands" she murmured...

Softly I say: "Mother, stop it, you mustn't think about it any more..." and yet I want to hear it...

For a while she sits staring in front of her and it is as if she is looking with eyes that do not see anything or maybe she is looking somewhere deep into herself; and suddenly I hear her voice as if it comes from very far and she says:

"When we came out in the morning we saw the ground wet and blood stained. Shreds of clothing were hanging in the electric barbed wire...The gypsy camp was extinct...You know, Son, we were used to seeing those slovenly people hanging about in their camp, in the evening we often heard them singing melancholy songs...those warm gypsy songs full of sentiment and we were so used to seeing their dark faces when we went to the plant in the morning and when we came back in the evening.

"All night long we heard the screaming and the clanging of the swords they were slaughtered with, the women and the children...All night long their screaming and in the morning that awful silence, which went to the bone.

"I am no human being, I have no blood, I have no heart, I am a camera, I see pictures. I see fighting devils, Germans, who thrust their swords into women and children, everywhere blood is gushing. They are driven to the lethal chambers, hundreds at the time. They already knew the gas chambers, they knew where they were going to."

The neighbors next door are playing music. "Silent Night, Holy Night"...Here I am writing about the thousands of gypsies of whom mother knows how they have been murdered. Here they are playing "Silent Night...Holy Night."

I have to dream away for a while. I remember how immediately after the war we hoped and dreamed about a more beautiful future. In each church, in each religion they prayed: Peace—never again war...

While I am dreaming away I see the picture of a lovely forest through which I once drove by car. All of a sudden I arrived at a glade and inquisitive like a child, I pushed the bushes a bit aside and through an opening I was looking at a gypsy camp. There sounded enchanting music and I while I saw how women were cooking in their caravans, I saw men chopping wood and making fire and all at once a young woman jumped forward and began to dance to the music like mad. Her body moved to the gripping tones of the music. Once more the gypsies dance, after thousands of them have been massacred...Once more the violins weep and like a sort of weed that grows luxuriantly, children once more are procreated and born, and everybody thinks: "Life is worth living..."

If you would like to go on listening to my fairy tale, then I must tell you how I have recently met a friend of my father...This happened by accident through my son and their conversation about surnames, during which ours was mentioned.

It gave me a very strange feeling to look into the eyes of a man who had looked into the eyes of my father 30 years ago, who had heard his voice and who was moved when he began to tell about our house, which he called the "Open House". I was glad to find that my fairy tale had not been a dream, everything was true. Really true. He described the atmosphere, which I remember so well. The open-door weekends with the stream of people walking in and out, filling the house with their jokes and laughs, singing songs together, such as "Leise fleeën meine Lieder"..."durch die Nacht zu dir"..., drinking tea, eating kümmel-bread with sausages, or nibbling biscuits, peeling nuts and everywhere there were round dishes with sweets. People kept hanging about for a while, talking about politics, little scandals, market reports, chatting about the weather, births and death They left in a happy mood, for they had been in a friendly home...Our home. In myself I still call our house "the dreamhouse". Because that is what it was. You could play in it! In the garden you could build castles of mud; catch rain worms, caterpillars and snails; you could throw mud-pancakes against the whitewashed walls. You could climb into the pear tree to play Red Indians...You could pick white and purple lilacs to ornament yourself; you could play at hide-and-seek in the wardrobes and cops-and-robbers somewhere among the beds. You could go and lie on them or creep under them. You were allowed to do everything. So you could rush through the hall with dirty feet, and you could bring in your friends without being checked. It did not matter what color they were, what race, rank or class; and there was always Babbe, who slipped something sweet into our hands, wiped our snotty noses and washed our hot heads with cold water. And mother who joined us in skipping and "Antoinette who's got the ball, turn around and then you'll know". And how we hung on her lips when she recited poems like: "He opened the little slide…and the gunner: mighty……and little hare sat in the ripe corn, nibbling the green grass…little hare, little hare look out!" In those times you could be nothing but happy!

And when you consider that that same mother, who had been skipping then…died on 1 September 1968, hardly 56 years old, as a result of the indescribable suffering in Auschwitz, Bergen-Belsen and Ravensbrück.

When you consider what her eyes must have seen and her heart must have felt once, then it is no wonder that the fairy tale ends here, for out of my eyes the tears are flowing, trickling down my cheeks and mouth and it is getting misty and dim before my eyes so that I cannot go on writing any more.

ONE STEP AHEAD
OF THE GERMANS
Szaja Lida

By Reba Karp

"It's hard to believe in God," Holocaust survivor Szaja Lida said, wondering where the divine presence was when the Jews were victimized by the Germans.

But then he pauses and explains the "other side of the coin." The Jews gave the civilized world, its civilized life, he added, noting that *The Bible* is still revered and Hitler's *Mein Kampf* is now only an example of unrestrained demogoguery.

Szaja's odyssey through the horrors of the Third Reich is one which took him from Crakow, Poland in 1939 to work camps, concentration camps, ammunition factories and finally to liberation in 1945. His exploits were that of a survivor, one determined to endure in spite of the odds and live to spit in the face of the devil.

The war touched Szaja and his family in 1939. He was 26 years old. "The Germans attacked at midnight," he remembers. "And everyone able to run, ran. We didn't know where we were going, we were just running." After three days his mother and younger sister couldn't run any more and returned home. But Szaja and brother-in-law continued to search for sanctuary as the situation was more threatening for Jewish men.

They were on the move for seven days and during that time could not find any water, for the wells had run dry due to the demands of thousands of people running from an unknown fate. "We were able to buy food...no one was concerned about who was Jewish then," he said.

While on the run, he was introduced to the specter of death, for at one point a German plane gunned down the helpless civilians. He was not on the road at the time. It would be the first of many narrow escapes and he would learn to survive.

Later, when conscripted off the road by German soldiers to help construct a road adjacent to a bridge, he learned another fact of aggression. The Jewish people of Poland had no legal rights, and as such were subjected to stop and search and seizure of all personal property and money. He would also learn to outwit the Germans.

It was after the road was finished and the Germans released him that he realized that he had no place to run and he began his weary trek back to Crakow. When he reached home, he found his family still alive, despite the fact that each house had some dead. (Before the war the Lida family owned a factory where underwear was produced. The Germans took over the business and later closed it down entirely.)

Although there were no ghettos in Poland between the two wars, the Jews still lived together in specific communities then, which made it easier for the Germans in the beginning. He recalls one morning when their neighborhood was searched by 25 or 30 German soldiers, "two or three in every home," he noted for he has a mind for details. "We didn't know what they wanted, they knocked you down if you asked." But the attack on the defenseless Jewish community was for search and seizure of valuables. But the Lidas were prepared, despite the uncertainty of the event, and had placed German marks in a nightstand and within easy search "so they would look no further."

They had outwitted the Germans, but some of their neighbors were not so lucky for many had nothing for the Germans and were subsequently abused and humiliated.

One of the first overt acts of anti-Semitism was the forced wearing of the Star of David. Later the Jewish people were not supposed to use any mode of transportation, and still later they were restricted from walking on the sidewalk. Those who disobeyed and were caught were beaten, he said.

Later restrictions prohibited the Jews from leaving town, which was necessary in order to trade for food as Polish currency had become devaluated. Recently established ghettos designed to hold 10,000 were filled to 60,000.

During 1941-42, Szaja and other young men worked for the Germans, loading grain, drying out wetlands. "The SS officers could not believe Jews could do such good work," he said, adding that despite hard work "everyday someone was dragged home, beaten."

In view of the encroaching hostility and constant threat to their family, the Lidas got permission to leave Crakow and returned to the small town where their grandparents had lived. "I rented a one-room apartment. I was lucky I got it…and we loaded everything we could in a truck and left."

He describes the move as one being "from hell to paradise," for the Crakow German headquarters had outlawed the Jewish people. They were no longer recognized as human beings and could be killed without explanation. They spent the winter of 1941-42 in the small town, which, before the war, had about 100 Jews. It now held close to 600 Jewish people who fled from the sealing of ghettos in other Polish cities and a sure "death sentence."

While living in the shtetl, Szaja became a member of the Judenrein, those of the Jewish community who acted as the intermediaries between the people and the Germans. He was at the headquarters when the news arrived that all Jews were to be assembled on the streets at 7 o'clock on a Monday morning. It was Sunday night. The order was delivered by SS officers carrying two slips of paper. One was the notice for every Jew to be ready to leave; and the other was a note asking extortion money—money to be used for transportation, feeding of the soldiers and for the use of "tools"—bullets to shoot the Jews. "And we had to pay for it," he remembers.

There was no way out and no way in, and yet the Lidas were to outwit the Nazis again. Szaja hid his family Sunday night in a neighbor's pile of hay. In the morning, he took his place with the Judenrein and watched helplessly as they first carted off the elderly to a cemetery where they were shot and dumped into already prepared graves. Then the rest were loaded on wagons and taken to the railroad station 20 kilometers away for the journey to Auschwitz.

Finally, the Germans searched the homes for those too sick to leave. It was quick and methodical. Those found were shot. Szaja and other Judenrein were given the job of taking the bodies to the cemetery and digging graves for them. He glanced sadly over the graves of the elderly shot earlier. "The dirt was still moving—24 hours later," he said, unable to hold back his emotions. They buried the dead as ordered and said kaddish out of respect.

"Forty years ago and it seems like it is happening now." His eyes were full of tears.

Then a new dimension in the battle for survival began for Szaja and his family. He took them food each night until he thought it safe for them to return to their home. Others who had hidden also returned, and just before the Germans were to remove those remaining, the Lidas hid again—this time in the attic of a Polish farmer. This sanctuary only lasted eight days, until the farmer noted that he had found a place where they could live in peace until the end of the war.

"He left us in the middle of a field in the frost, cold..."

They knocked on neighboring doors, begging help. "All we received were curses," from the Christians. Legally they were supposed to be dead, for all that had lived in the shtetl were gone. Their entire world had become hostile. Exposed to the cold and with no food, they decided they would go to Crakow and take their chances in the ghetto, and in order to assure a better chance at reaching their destination, the family separated on the train. Szaja was sitting close to a Jewish woman and her two children when the Germans caught them, and took them off the train and shot them. He was overlooked. But his heart was heavy—another young Jewish woman and her children were dead.

Since he was a young man and would be shot upon entering the ghetto, he parted with his family and moved through the hostile elements of Crakow. "Every step my life was in danger. No Jews were allowed to live outside." He found his way to a work camp where he saw two of his friends and with their help moved in with the workers, avoiding the regular entrance channels where all valuables were taken away.

The workers were given only 500 calories of food a day, but his valuables managed to "buy" additional food for his friends and himself. These friends are still alive, living in Tennessee, he said. Although he caught typhus and nearly died, he was given a chance to recuperate by the Austrian camp official, interested in lowering the number of those who died in his camp or who became too ill to work and was subsequently shot. "If only they had enough food, they would have been the best workers. But they killed them."

In the winter of 1943, the surviving workers were loaded on trains for a seven hour trip to an ammunition factory. Since he knew his life depended upon having something to sell, in exchange for food, he changed clothes with another worker who was dressed in little more than rags—and once more outwitted the Germans, who, disdainful of his clothes, did not thoroughly search him.

Conditions at the factory were inhumane. One camp produced chemicals to make mines, which turned the workers' skin and hair yellow. "No one lived longer than a month. There was so much hunger...some wore paper bag clothes, shoes...and the warehouse was full of clothes from the Jewish dead."

Food consisted of a plate of dirty water. "If someone found a piece of potato, the whole camp knew." And because of the conditions, the number of workers never exceeded 2,500, despite the fact that they brought in 500 new workers each month. No one was shot. They died of starvation.

Szaja was assigned to loading heavy empty shells from a train en route to the factory. The shells weighed between 80 and 90 pounds and were beyond his physical ability to carry. After several weeks, "I knew I would not make it," he said, explaining that the procedure was to carry the shells over one shoulder. "They wore through my heavy overcoat, jacket and shirt to the shoulder"...which had become bruised and bloodied.

He had to gain time and sought a way to survive and found the weak link—the Polish manager the Germans had put in charge. He was an alcoholic and Szaja offered him money for a quart of vodka if he would find him another place to work. The man agreed and he was assigned to loading smaller, empty shells into the factory for others to fill, a job which kept him one step ahead of the specter of death.

Cut off from communications, the only clues as to what was happening in the outside world, were events surrounding the camp. A signal that the war was going badly for the Germans occurred in April 1944, when work crews were forced into the forests to exhume and burn the bodies of workers previously killed. "The stench was overpowering," he remembers. The work crews never returned.

Before the camp was closed in June 1944, a breakout was planned. He held back, despite the fact that the camp was buzzing with intrigue. Two of his friends decided to join the escapees. He warned them against it, reminding them that the woods were infested with Germans. Each 10 feet of forest contained either Germans or ammunition. I asked them, "Do you think we can break through?"

His friends went as far as the fence and then decided to return. Half of the camp escaped that night. They cut the wire fence and by 7 or 8 a.m. that next morning, the Germans had already caught 100 of them. "All were caught except two...and all were shot in front of us," he said.

Before the camp was closed "selections" were made. "Those with nothing to wear were considered the weakest" and were subsequently shot. He remembers a mother begging for the life of her 15-year-old daughter. The SS officer responded by shooting both of them. And then he remembers another horror. As those who had been selected to be shot were being led away, they begged, not for their lives, but for a piece of bread—their hunger was so intense.

The next day, he found himself on a train for Buchenwald. Each prisoner received a half loaf of bread, a little margarine and marmalade. There were about 100 in each train car, "and hardly room to stand." By the time the train reached its destination, after picking up more prisoners along the way, there were 3,000 human souls on board. Once unloaded they were confronted by four crematoriums and the stench of burning human flesh.

As they waited to be admitted to the camp, few thought they would survive, for they had to wait under the ominous threat and smoke and stench of the crematorium.

However, Szaja held on to a fragment of hope, feeling that if the Germans wanted them dead, they would not have gone through all the trouble of transporting them to Buchenwald. He tried to bolster the spirits of those around him.

He was right, but once into the admitting quarters, he was finally forced to part with his remaining item of value—a piece of gold chain. But he still tried to think ahead. He divided what was left among his friends and pushed his share into a piece of soap, which he stuffed into his boots.

After quarantine, the workers were sent to a village near Berlin to work in an ammunition factory producing anti-tank grenades. They worked on two shifts—12 hours each. The food he describes as being "too much to die and not enough to live."

There were acts of courage—and desperation at this camp as the war began to wind down. One involved a boy who had been badly beaten by a German who threatened to kill him if he didn't show up for work the next day. Of course, it would have been impossible, he said, so out of desperation, the boy started a fire in the factory.

"None came out alive. All was destroyed."

But in less than three months, the plant was rebuilt, with the help of the cruel Hitler Youth Corps. The months dragged on and close to April the factory was closed forever. In typical German Teutonic fashion the prisoners were ordered to clean up the factory so that the approaching Russians would find it in order! Each prisoner was given a pack of cigarettes for his labor...the first Szaja had had in three years.

Once more he was shoved on a train, this time the destination was Theresenstadt. Except for a half loaf of bread and a stick of margarine, they had no food for days and no water. Incredibly, before he left he was given back his old clothes and the boots with the soap and piece of gold chain!

The Germans were losing and the tracks were heavy with traffic, forcing the train to stop every 20 minutes. "People started to die...we didn't know what to do with the bodies...we lined them up around the edges and used them as pillows."

Finally, they reached a large station where cars were loaded with rutabagas, the first and only food they had had in days. The dead were carried away by borrowed horses and wagons, and the prisoners were expected to bury them. "We were so weak we couldn't dig more than two feet a day."

After eight or nine more days of a diet restricted to rutabagas, more began to die. Once more the Germans stopped the train and borrowed shovels and wagons to bury the dead. Some escaped at this point. The soldiers did not seem to care. Szaja estimates that he was on the train for 24 days before they arrived at Theresenstadt, where they found the German guards had disappeared. The camp was left to operate on its own and once more he was put into quarantine.

Getting enough food was a problem, and as he walked through the camp he noticed a group of people who were in special enclosures. These were the converts…Jews of and from intermarriages with Germans. He climbed over the fence and approached an elderly woman who asked him to help her move her belongings in exchange for old bread, obviously rations she had stored away. Other elderly women also asked his help and "by night I had my belly full and…three bags of bread," which he threw over the fence and shared with those who had continued to sit in the barracks because "they couldn't find anything to eat."

Liberation was a little less than they expected, it consisted merely of a Russian who was passing through who opened the gates and told them they were free. "Later the Red Cross came and disinfected us, bathed us and weighed us." After two weeks of eating the bread shared by the elderly mishlings, Szaja weighed 66 pounds. His weight at the beginning of the war was 170 pounds.

Liberation was not without its irony. Before the Red Cross arrived, some of the prisoners had pillaged nearby towns for food. Szaja warned them to eat only staples such as bread, potatoes, rice, that their systems would be unable to tolerate rich foods. Those who did not heed his warnings developed dysentery and died. "Hundreds…thousands died this way. The streets were filled with human waste and people lying in the waste…half the camp died after liberation."

The joy of liberation was further marred for Szaja, who remembers the busses sent by countries to pick up their citizens. "But none came from Poland. Our hearts were broken, everything was lost." Later he returned to his home and it was "like going back to a cemetery. We were told to leave," he said.

"I asked myself, did it pay to be left over? I left and never returned."

Today he is a retired grocery merchant who lives with his wife in Virginia. He has one daughter, Anna Lida Karp, who also lives in Virginia.

A STORY OF COURAGE, CUNNING AND INTRIGUE
Kitty Saks

By Reba Karp

This is a story which might not have been written if three desperate Jews had not bribed officials in Brussels, Belgium in 1940 to be put on the list of those scheduled to leave early in May of that year.

The threesome took the place of Edith and Leo Friedenbach and their daughter Kitty. As a consequence, the Friedenbachs were put on another list. Their new date of departure was May 15, 1940. The Germans marched in on May 10, 1940.

The Friedenbachs' story is one of courage, cunning and intrigue, made possible only because, unlike the Poles, the Belgians, as a rule, were not overly anti-Semitic. As Kitty Friedenbach Saks says today: "They (Belgians) would help their fellow human beings, although there were some who lacked that human respect."

Kitty traces her family's anguish in World War II back to 1939 when it became apparent that with the approach of the Germans, the Jewish population would be in jeopardy. Kitty was born in Vienna where she lived with her parents and grandparents. Her father was a fruit merchant; her grandfather, a retired jeweler. "My mother was a musician and piano teacher. We lived with my grandparents in a very nice apartment overlooking the Danube Canal," she said.

Memories of the apartment are overshadowed with bitterness. The home she remembers so fondly was "confiscated" by an officer in the Wehrmacht. "He walked into my grandparents' apartment...on a Shabbat evening. He looked around and liked what he saw. He liked the apartment, the furnishings, the view. I remember my grandmother had just lit the Shabbat candles and we were ready to sit down to dinner.

"He told my grandparents that he would personally see that they were resettled in another apartment. What choice did they have?"

Shortly after that "intrusion" Kitty and her parents began their elaborate attempts to get over the border into Belgium. Her grandparents decided to stay behind because he was a veteran of the Austrian army of World War I. "He thought that perhaps he would be exempt, that he would be able to live in Vienna. Of course, that proved to be untrue," she said. Her grandparents were among the first to perish in experiments with gas in trucks.

Leo Friedenbach crossed the border first, but not because he put his life before that of his family. "We knew that they took the men first and dispatched them to labor camps. I believe Buchenwald was at that time under construction."

The procedure to leave Vienna before the Germans was elaborate but was made possible for Kitty and her family by the fact they had cousins in Norfolk, Harry and Margie Coplon. "My father stood in line many many nights just to get to the authorities, to have his name put on the list so that we would be able to leave Vienna, all of us.

"However, the doors were always slammed just before he got to the front of the line."

The alternate route across the border was to hire a guide and take risks. But again, she explains, "What choice did we have?"

During those pre-dawn days of the concentration camps, word among desperate men traveled quickly and through dangerous routes. Mercenaries willing to help those wishing to escape would gather in Aachen, a small town on the border, at the Schloss Hotel. There, for a price, refugees could buy their attempt to cross the border to Belgium or France, countries yet unoccupied by the Germans.

Her father made it on the first try and sent word for Kitty and her mother to follow. "We left in April of 1939 and made it to Aachen and to the famous Schloss Hotel." The trip from Vienna to Aachen was only the beginning of a nerve-wracking seven attempts to cross the border—a woman, alone, with a small child.

"Once we were spotted by searchlights and turned back. On another try, the guide on the Belgian side failed to appear at the appointed time and place," she said, explaining that the effort was a joint one which had to be coordinated on both sides. "Still on another occasion, and after being caught and detained at the checkpoint building, we were stripped and searched. This was a painful embarrassment to my mother, who was a very proper person. She was even more upset that I, a 6-year-old, was so treated." This time they were turned back due to some irregularity in their papers and also because a fellow refugee was remembered from a previous attempt to cross the border. The fellow refugee was detained and "we never saw him again." At that point, Belgium seemed a far and distant place to Kitty's mother, who as a woman, was more vulnerable to the vicissitudes of the guides and border patrol.

They tried again, this time with a woman as their guide. Her plan was to pretend that they were heading for a picnic near the border. But that attempt proved to be another bitter disappointment, for just as they had convinced the guards of their "innocent" intentions, another voice called out "Halt!" and added sarcastically, "Sie wollen uber die grune gene," (You want to go over to the green, i.e., beautiful, yearned for border). Yes, they did…but it was back to Aachen and the Schloss Hotel!

"'Here comes Friedenbach with the kid,' still rings in my ears" she added. "It was becoming a joke."

Time was working against them. The money and valuables they had brought with them from Vienna were all but gone. "But we planned ahead for just such an emergency," Kitty said. "My mother phoned my grandparents who wired money. The prearranged code was 'tante ist sehr krank.' " ("Auntie is very sick," which told Kitty's grandparents, that they didn't make it; send money.)

The days at the Schloss Hotel were full of intrigue, as desperate men and women maneuvered and bargained with guides. Although only 6-years-old at the time, Kitty sensed the enormity of the situation. Alone with her mother much of the time, she could feel the fear. "We had no choice but to keep trying. We knew the alternative. Crossing the border was a great risk to all—including the guides."

That a heavy toll was required was understandable, she reasons, as she recalls their last and successful attempt. "My mother noticed that the guide had been drinking heavily. She voiced doubts about his ability to get us across in his condition.

"His response was that *only in this* condition would he do the job."

It was a cold April night in the woods between Aachen and the Belgium border. On a previous crossing in January, a child had frozen to death right in the arms carrying him across. "They rubbed and massaged me all night long, giving me what warmth they could."

Once across the border, in Eupen-Malmedy, the exhausted party was given warmth and breakfast at a prearranged farm house where they were joined by another group of those fleeing the Nazis. Then they left by train for Brussels where they were joined by her father. They had a few moments of joy at the reunion; but it was sobered by the thoughts of their next great effort—getting to America, an attempt which was thwarted by another's bargaining with the officials.

Then the Germans marched in. Soon after, a law was passed that no Jewish child could attend school. Unaware, Kitty and her friend Mela, displaying their compulsory big yellow star, walked into class. "Much to our shock when we entered, the teacher asked us what we were doing in school. We were allowed to remain for the day, but we had to sit behind the stove." That was the last day Kitty attended a public school in Belgium.

"My physical education teacher at that time was a woman by the name of Femande Henrard. She was a saint, a true heroine of the war. At great risk to herself, she saved hundreds of Jewish children by placing them in convents. She saw me one day running an errand for my parents. She stopped me with the warning:'Don't you know that it is dangerous for you to be walking the streets with your star? They (Germans) will pick you up and then your parents will be picked up.' She told me she had a plan, for my parents to come to see her."

That night they met with Mademoiselle Henrard and she explained her plan to place Kitty in a convent school as a Catholic, under an assumed name. "Of course, my father objected at first, but later he gave me his last 50 francs to save me. There was no other way." (Kitty's parents were expected to pay a stipend to the convent for the room and board.) "But this was minimal," she added, explaining that once when her parents did not have the money, her mother gave the school her gold wedding band.

"I was 9-years-old at the time and it sounded exciting," Kitty said. However, it was easier said than done, for Mademoiselle Henrard had to try several convent schools before she could find a place for Kitty.

"The nuns explained their reluctance. It would be dangerous to all if they were discovered hiding a Jewish child, for the Germans would kill everyone connected with the school—Catholic children as well as the nuns." With each try, Kitty would accompany Mademoiselle Henrard to the different schools. Since she was allowed to return to her parents after each thwarted attempt, she viewed it as a grand play.

But Mademoiselle Henrard persisted, as she did many times for many Jewish children. Finally, Paridaens, a convent in Louvain, a Catholic boarding elementary/secondary school, accepted her. She was enrolled under the assumed name of Rosette Nizole, deceased niece of a priest. "It was necessary for my parents to sign a document giving permission for the school to give me Catholic training and to baptize me. Not to partake in religious instruction and activities would have quickly aroused suspicion."

It was a momentous day in her life and memories still ring through her mind as distinctly as the bell which rang to open the convent door. "We were ushered into a gigantic waiting room. When the doors banged shut, I knew I would not be back with my parents that night."

The new friends, new name and new identity were not as formidable as the new surroundings which were so foreign to her Jewish upbringing. Crucifixes in place of menorahs, Latin liturgies in place of davening Hebrew; she was a long way from home. "I cried myself to sleep that night."

Kitty learned the sacraments and was baptized "under great ceremony" secretly in a side chapel. One of the sisters who knew about it, made Kitty a white dress for the occasion. "I understood why it was necessary, that my parents had to sign to save me. But I also knew that I was Jewish and I was proud of my heritage. After being baptized and learning my catechism backward and forward, I continued to say 'Sh'ma,' the traditional Jewish prayer of faith, privately every night in secret."

In order to succeed, Mademoiselle Henrard had to think of everything. Small details were important, for one endangered child could alert the Germans and endanger them all. During holidays and vacations, when the Catholic girls went home, Kitty was placed in orphanages for she could no longer return safely to her parents. The orphanages were in great contrast to the convent schools. Conditions were poor—hunger, malnutrition, cold and disease. "One summer vacation I was taken to Institute St. Charles in the Ardennes, where there were several other Jewish children. One of our daily chores was to pick worms out of the mattress stuffing. It was not my favorite activity."

But she managed to survive each "vacation," to return to Paridaens, which by comparison seemed as a paradise. Although Kitty's parents did not know where she was, she was kept informed on their general condition by Mademoiselle Henrard or her associate, who one day told her that the Gestapo had visited the building where her parents were hiding, but that they were okay.

Kitty later learned that it was only a capricious twist of fate which had spared her parents. The much-frightened Friedenbachs heard the Gestapo enter the building from their small quarters on the fourth floor. Her father was in bed at the time, a bed supported by heavy springs which groaned and loudly creaked with every turn of the body. The Gestapo got as far as the fourth floor, pulling people out as they progressed. They stopped in front of her parents' door. It was only held closed by a small latch. They pounded and the latch strained. Forced, out of fear, to remain perfectly still on the bed, his eyes warned Kitty's mother across the room not to move. They remained frozen in fear, daring not to breathe, as the Germans banged once more with their boots against the door. The fragile lock held again. At this moment, the landlady downstairs shouted up at the Germans that the people living in the apartment were Austrians with work permits who were out working. This sounded reasonable and reluctantly they left.

Kitty reasons now that they did not persist because of this and the fact that they already had a carload of helpless humans.

Before the Gestapo returned, and they did, her parents sought refuge in another apartment building. It was later learned that the Jews picked up in the building had been sold out by Belgians for 500 francs each. "But they lost 1,500 francs because I wasn't there and my parents escaped."

When Kitty learned of the near disaster she begged permission to go see her parents in their new hiding place. At first, for her safety, she was refused. But she persisted. Finally, they relented and Henrard's assistant, Mademoiselle Esther, took her as far as one block from her parent's quarters.

"I had to go the last stretch alone." It seemed like such a long block. The surroundings were new and she felt so small and alone. Although only about 10-years-old at the time, she had maturity beyond her years. Jewish children were forced to grow up fast in Europe. Then she ran into what she terms "potential disaster," for just outside her parents' building, she met one of her old girlfriends. "Her parents were known Nazi sympathizers and she knew, of course, that I was Jewish. We greeted each other with 'bonjour' and I entered. An awful scenario flashed through my mind of all of us being denouced; the Gestapo seizing us and deporting us to some unknown but suspected horror.

"But nothing happened. Did she say something to her parents? Or did she just dismiss it from her mind as a casual meeting? I'll never know."

Once Kitty's parents were settled in their new hiding place, they were determined to be prepared for such surprise visits from the Gestapo. Her father devised a hiding place by partitioning off part of the room, which had a slanting roof, and covering it with wallpaper, the same pattern as was on the other walls of the room. The opening for ventilation was under the bed which was up against the false wall. The wallpaper was carefully chosen to give the room a larger appearance so no one would suspect the presence of a false wall, she said. Fortunately, they never had to use the room.

Her parents managed to stay alive while in hiding by making cigarettes for a German Jew who had a Gentile spouse. Tobacco was distributed to the Jews in hiding, who had special machines to make the cigarettes. They were also provided with boxes to package the finished products, which were later sold on the Black Market to the German Wehrmacht.

Of course, Kitty explained, there was little profit in it for the Jews in hiding, who out of necessity had become cheap labor. Once more her father's ingenuity provided him with a little extra sustenance, for he devised a way to cut down on the tobacco used by putting loose particles in the center and packing in firmer on the ends. The saved tobacco was used to make extra packs for his own sale later. These were distributed, espionage-fashion, to a man who had a special knock and special code.

"Of course, it was not a large amount, but enough to make ends meet for a couple days here and there. It was never enough, my parents always ran out of food; then there was the cold and the unsanitary conditions and the lack of freedom. They could not be seen on the streets. But they managed to survive."

Kitty was transferred from convent to convent; from orphanage to orphanage—each with stories of its own. During one shift, during Christmas vacation, when she was being introduced to the girls at a Malines orphanage in Belgium, she almost encountered disaster, and only quick thinking on her part helped her avoid it. There was another girl at the orphanage with the same name, Rosette Nizole.

"Quickly, I changed mine, I said my name was Laurant, which satisfied them, but I had to do some very fast thinking. Actually, my experiences in all the Catholic institutions was like being in a play where you had to make up your own words, your own part as you went along. There was just no other way."

She had to remember to speak French, not German and was once put on trial by her peers when she spoke a few German words in her sleep. "I thought fast again. I told them I had a German aunt who used to visit and that I learned a few words from her."

Toward the end of the war, Kitty had to be perceptive to all nuances, to take nothing at face value, for Mademoiselle Henrard and her associates had placed so many children that there was developing a lack of continuity. "She must have found it hard to keep up with all of us. Of course, she couldn't keep any written records."

Conditions at orphanages grew steadily worse. In a particular one, the girls all had severe skin infections, which was due in part, no doubt, to the fact that they were bathed only every two weeks and the procedure was to bathe 12 children in one bath water—outside. When she could endure no more, she went up to one of the Catholic sisters and implored her to let her be number five instead of number 10.

Mademoiselle Henrard later took her out of that particular orphanage. "I must have been her pet. She found another place for me, three blocks from my parents. They did not know where I was, but I knew where they were. She placed me with the Sisters of Charity of St. Vincent de Paul," Kitty remembers.

"Mademoiselle Esther used to visit my father to see how he was and he would beg her to tell him where I was. She would answer him with 'pas loin,' which means 'not far,' but she would not tell him where."

In the early days of September 1944, the British troops entered Brussels. They could hear the guns all night. "That morning of Sept. 4, 1944 at 9 o'clock, the doors swung open and one of the sisters came in and told us we were liberated. The unbelievable nightmare had ended. I can still hear the joyful words of one of the Catholic sisters: 'Mes enfants, nous somnes liberés'—my children, we are liberated!

"I asked permission to go to my parents, who I knew weren't far away. The mother superior told me I would have to wait until they contacted Mademoiselle Henrard and someone came to pick me up. Meanwhile, they dressed us so we could go see the British troops. When I returned, I learned that my parents had been at the convent looking for me.

"Then they packed a little bag for me to go to Mademoiselle Henrard, who was also only a short distance away. When I arrived at her home, she kissed me and said, 'Good luck. You know how to get home.' "

"I ran across the cobblestone streets all the way to my parents' apartment. I knocked on the door. I yelled! I screamed!

"My mother looked out of the window and cried: 'Kitty! Kitty!'

"I had come home to stay."

Kitty later learned that Mademoiselle Henrard had been earlier picked up by the Germans and questioned about her activities. "But she never revealed one name, *never!*" Kitty corresponded with Mademoiselle Henrard until her death in recent years. Understandably, Kitty would like to see Mademoiselle Henrard's name among those honored on the Avenue of the Righteous in Israel.

"I will also carry with me, in fondest memory and deepest gratitude the names of four nuns who cared for me during the most trying time of my life, Sister Marie Bernadette, Sister Marie Layola, Sister Marie Dominique and Sister Marie Michaels.

Kitty is married to Abbott Saks, chairman of the language department at Maury High School and a member of the evening faculty at Old Dominion University. They have two children; David, who is a doctor, and Antoine, a 1982 graduate of Old Dominion University.

ABOUT OUR CO-SPONSOR AND HIS WIFE: SURVIVAL IN AMERICA

Andrew Maurice Fekete was born in Norfolk, Virginia on July 28, 1929. His parents, Dora and Maurice Fekete, were Hungarian immigrants to the United States. Father Maurice died a few days after his son's birth due to an accident. Dora, by that time the mother of four children, acquired a grocery store in order to support her family. It is hard to imagine the struggle the widow underwent in those years.

Andrew, with much love and care from his mother, grew up into a fine young man. He had a burning desire to become a physician, following in the tradition of his Hungarian family. He graduated at 16 from Maury High School, attended the Norfolk Branch of The College of William and Mary (today Old Dominion University), went on to George Washington University in Washington, D.C., in order to find employment in a larger city to put himself through undergraduate school. After obtaining his B.S., he enrolled in the Medical College of Virginia. Years of intense struggle began. The Shriners granted him a loan to stay in school when matters seemed impossible. In his last year, apart from the many grueling hours, he held as many as seven part-time jobs.

He graduated in June 1956. Fekete and his new bride, the former Ruth Gelb of Philadelphia, moved to Norfolk for a residency in internal medicine at Norfolk General Hospital. Ruth worked until their first child, Janet, was born. Then the family survived on his meager salary.

In 1959 Andrew accepted a special residency at the Graduate Hospital in Philadelphia under Dr. Sam Bellet. Their residency was made possible by staying with Ruth's parents, during which time Ruth was pregnant with daughter, Sharon. But, nine months later, Andrew contracted hepatitis making it impossible to continue. As the hospital offered no insurance, they had to return to Norfolk in order to obtain unemployment insurance, which was conditional on his fulfilling his armed forces service obligations. As he was unable to serve, the family was stranded with two children and no income. A Norfolk hospital finally offered him a part-time position and several insurance companies used his services for medical physical examinations.

In 1961 he was finally able to open his own practice through the kindness of a fellow physician who shared his office with Andrew at no charge. Two years later, as his practice grew, he opened his own office, and moved the family into a small house. In 1965 Ruth gave birth to their son, David, and they built the home they live in now.

Ruth Fekete describes her husband as follows: "He has never forgotten from where he came and how hard it was to achieve his ambitions. He is probably one of the most sympathetic, charitable, and beautiful human beings I have ever known. He always gives when others need and feels when others hurt. His charitable nature far outweighs his financial ability to give. But he knows too well how it feels to need and could never stand by watching the needy without giving beyond his ability. I love him very much and I pray that God will give him the strength and the years to continue doing his best for his fellow man." (Mrs. Ruth Fekete was honored in 1985 by the Tidewater Jewish Federation for, among others, her activities on behalf of Holocaust survivors. She has given numerous hours to her commitment, and deserves deep-felt gratitude for her unstinting and excellent work.)

Dr. Andrew ("Andy") Fekete's background, coupled with his work-directed nature, (he is Medical Director of Lake Taylor Hospital,) has allowed him to branch out into an area of medicine which provides primary care for those needing minor emergency assistance, but cannot always afford their regular physician, or are unable to find one during the hours of their need.

Whatever Dr. Fekete's professional achievements are and will be, he is above all a "Mensch," the highest compliment all those who know him/of him can pay. The Publishers join his wife, their children and his many friends in wishing Andy many years of good personal health and health care for others.

BIBLIOGRAPHY

Allen, W.S. *The Nazi Seizure of Power*. New York: New Viewpoints, 1973.

Beuer, Yehuda. *The Holocaust in Historical Perrspective*. Seattle: Unitersity of Washington Press, 1978.

Berkovitz, Eliezer. *With God in Hell*. New York: Sanhedrin Press, 1979.

Dawidowicz, Lucy S. *A Holocaust Reader*. New York: Behrman House, 1976.

des Pres, Terrence. *The Survivor*. Oxford: Oxford University Press, 1976.

Donat, Alexander. *The Holocaust Kingdom*. New York: Holt, Reinhart and Winston, 1963.

Friedlander, Henry and Sybil Milton (Editors). *The Holocaust: Ideology, Bureaucracy and Genocide*. New York: Kraus International Publications, 1980.

Hellman, Peter. *Avenue of the Righteous*. New York: Atheneum, 1980.

Hillberg, Raul. *The Destruction of European Jews*. Chicago: Quadrangle Press, 1961.

Rabinowitz, Dorothy. *New Lives*. New York: Alfred A. Knopf, 1976.

Raske, Richard. *Escape from Sobibor*. Boston, MA: Houghton Mifflin Co.

Trunk, Isaiah. *Jewish Response to Nazi Persecution*. New York: Stein and Day, 1978.

Wiesenthal, Simon. *The Sunflower*. New York: Schocken, 1976.